EXPLODE:

The Proven System to Sell 500 Homes a Year While Keeping a Balanced Life

Rhyan Finch

EXPLODE: The Proven System to Sell 500 Homes a Year While Keeping a Balanced Life

Copyright © 2015 by Rhyan Finch.

Disclaimer & FTC Notice

Neither the author nor the publisher assumes any responsibility or liability whatsoever on the behalf of the purchaser or reader of these materials.

Any perceived slight of any individual or organization is purely unintentional.

Foreword

Success is not just about money. Money may help us keep score along the way, but most of us want more. We want the sense of fulfillment that comes from achieving our dreams and changing the lives of others for the better. This book can help you make a lot of money, but more importantly, it can help you find that kind of satisfaction.

When I founded Liberty Tax Service eighteen years ago, we didn't have much money. We were competing against one of the strongest brands in the United States (H&R Block), as well as against a company that bore my name (Jackson Hewitt). Everyone said we were crazy to try to break into that market, but I decided that it was the right thing to do. This new venture was my passion, and I knew I had to follow where it led.

Since then, I have been named the Entrepreneur of the Year by the International Franchise Association, Entrepreneur of the Year for the State of

Virginia and one of the Most Influential People in Accounting fourteen years in a row. The accolades the company has received are too numerous to mention here.

When you have worked so hard to achieve such a seemingly impossible goal, it is rare to encounter someone who shares your level of passion. But that is what I see in Rhyan Finch. I have watched him on his journey from a rookie agent to one of the top brokers in the nation. He has tackled every phase with boundless energy and enthusiasm. And like me, he has always wanted to do more than make money; he too has worked to build a company that is changing people's lives for the better.

Explode will help you master the fundamentals of real estate, grow your business and keep your life in balance. Very few people are willing to talk honestly about their mistakes, let alone share the secrets of their road to success. Those who do take genuine delight in the success of others. Fortunately for anyone who wants to succeed in real estate, Rhyan

Finch is such a person, as you will see in the pages that follow.

-John Hewitt

Founder, Chairman

and CEO of Liberty Tax

Table of Contents

Introduction

I've been told "no" in my life more times than I can count.

"No, Rhyan. We don't need you on the team."

I loved sports growing up, but I was short and scrawny. I didn't make the all-stars for Little League. I sat on the bench in football. When I did go in at wide receiver, I knew it was going to be a running play. I was the only kid in my high school to be cut from the baseball team. I tried wrestling, but I didn't win a single match my first year.

"No, Rhyan. We don't think college is for you."

My professional life didn't get off to a much better start than my athletic career. My granddad got me a job at an HVAC company, but I was fired. They didn't think I had what it took to learn the profession. Like many teenagers from ordinary families, I worked minimum wage jobs through high school. At eighteen, someone I trusted cleaned out my bank account, and I got evicted from my home. While all my friends were going off to college, I found myself with no place to live, no money in my bank account and living away from where I'd grown up.

My Aunt Kelly took me in, even though she really didn't have the space and had her own family to care for. I worked two jobs until I could get a small place of my own in low income housing. But at age twenty, I found myself jobless.

Backed to the wall, I made some decisions I'm not proud of. I even resorted to selling drugs, and I'm grateful to this day that I didn't get into more trouble. Looking back on it, I should be dead or in jail. Like a lot of young men with a thin support system and little education, I felt stuck. I knew I wanted to make something of myself, and I wasn't afraid of working hard. But what could I do?

Real estate was the answer I was looking for.

"Yes, Rhyan, we'll give you a shot."

Real estate offered me an opportunity to learn and grow, and ultimately to give my family the kind of life I'd always wanted for them. It was a very bumpy road at first, but I knew I'd found where I belonged. From selling four homes my first month to selling 900 homes in 2012, real estate showed me what was possible, not just in business, but also in life. Going from selling drugs to selling the Dream. Going from homeless to home-selling hero it felt like. Thanks to our success, we've helped thousands of homeowners and provided jobs and opportunities to many wonderful individuals.

If you've never worked in real estate, this book will show you what is possible. Maybe you're stuck in a job you don't love or doesn't allow you the flexibility to be with your family. Or maybe your job isn't paying you enough to give your children the opportunities you want for them. This book will teach you how to succeed in the industry while having enough time for the people who matter most to you.

I have seen too many talented, motivated agents go under or give up without realizing their full potentials. I don't want to see another person make the jump into this profession without realizing their dreams. Maybe you're already working as an agent or a team leader, but you can't seem to gain any momentum. Or you might be making six figures, but you know there's more you can accomplish. If you know you have the drive to build something bigger than what you have—a team, a brokerage, or a franchise—this book will give you the mindset and tools for the journey.

This is not a comprehensive guide that tells you everything there is to know about real estate. There are plenty of great books out there that will explain every term and rule you can imagine. This book is a road map to selling 500 homes a year, while living a balanced life. After all, what is the point of financial success if you don't have the time to enjoy it?

In this book you'll learn that you don't have to be in a particular market or locality to make it work; you just have to be willing to learn and grow. I've also provided additional resources in the appendices to help you *Explode* your business.

This book tells the story of how real estate changed my life and allowed me to make a positive difference in the lives of others. I'm not peddling abstract theories but proven approaches that have worked across the country. Everything I recommend is something I've done myself and am still doing today.

Real estate is not the only way to be successful, but it is a way that can work for almost anyone. I am so thankful for what I have been able to do and am still doing in this industry, and it is my passion to help as many people as I can along the way.

Chapter 1:

The Evolution of a Real Estate Agent

Selling real estate changed my life.

In just a few years, I went from being a plumber struggling to raise my daughter alone to a member of Re/Max's Diamond Award Club. I went from doing 30 deals in 2006 to 900 deals in 2012 with a team average of well over 500 deals per year from 2010 through 2014. Starting out as a rookie agent, I became the leader of a 21-member team and then finally opened my own brokerage and real estate company. We doubled our volume of sales every year for six consecutive years, all during one of the worst markets in the history of real estate.

But I almost didn't make it. I was struggling in traditional re-sales and short sales, ready to go under, when I landed a huge Real Estate Owned (REO) account. In a matter of weeks, I had to hire like crazy, reorganize my entire business and learn a brand new system. But within a year, I was running multiple offices across the state. Within two years, I had offices all over the country. In short, my business *Exploded.*

There are a lot of real estate books out there. I know, because I've read most of them. One thing I noticed as I read is that, more often than not, the authors were not actually using the systems or strategies they described. Some are out of the business entirely by the time their books become popular. Others are primarily motivational speakers or coaches. They use their experience in real estate as a platform, but most haven't actually achieved the volume of business they promise to readers. Some may have done it in one market but found coaching more lucrative.

Early on in my career, I learned a lot about real estate that wasn't in those books. My lessons came from late nights, and lots of trial and error. But it wasn't until I had done 900 transactions in a year that anyone else was interested in what I had to say about it. By the grace of God, I have actually done what my book describes: I have sold 500 homes a year, and I have a balanced life. Not only that, I'm still doing it, and so can you.

What Does Success Look Like?

Most real estate classes have about 30 students. Typically, the brokerage running the class sets the students' expectations very low, warning them that they may not sell a house for six months or more. After paying all their upfront fees, the new agents that do sell homes will normally sell them to friends and family members. A year later, only a couple agents have sold enough to quit their day jobs, while the rest have probably given up.

Some brokerages simply run their businesses this way. They have a class of 30 students every month or two, let those new agents sell to their friends and family members (while the company collects the bulk of the commission) and then they start again with a new group. They never teach those agents how to enlarge their spheres of influence to be successful, because they know there will always be another crop in the door next month.

In a brokerage with low value splits, the agents who do sell will soon figure out that they could be making a lot more money out on their own. Many will decide to start their own teams rather than split commissions with a brokerage that doesn't seem to be doing much for them. These are typically the people who possess the skills and drive to be extremely successful in the business, but if they don't choose their next steps wisely, they can run out of money very quickly.

So how do you succeed in real estate instead of going broke trying? There is a way to *Explode* if you plan well from the beginning. Here is a brief overview of the process:

1. Start With Buyers

You cannot jump into real estate on your own if you don't understand how the business actually works. You must pay your dues, ideally as part of a healthy, profitable team that will reward you well for your labor. This is especially important if you are new to an area. You'll have people to answer your questions, and your team leader will be spending the money to generate leads. The cost per lead actually goes down in a team situation, because the team leader is "buying in bulk," paying to generate a lot of leads at once.

If you're ambitious, you may want to skip this step. But remember, it doesn't have to take forever. I only spent a year on a team before I went out on my own, but the information I learned and the experiences I gained that year are priceless. Everything you will gain in your time on a functional team will serve you well for the rest of your life. Think of your time as a team agent as paid career training. Make sure that the team allows you the opportunity to be mentored by someone who is at least a few steps ahead of you in the process, while also providing you with the leads and support staff that you need to be a successful buyers' agent. Even if you decide to start in real estate on your own, you should have a mentor who has been successful in the business.

In some models, the broker will mentor you directly. In larger brokerages, experienced agents will help new agents. Be sure to ask how much access you will have to the person who will be involved in your professional development; you need to have enough time so your mentor can show you the ropes and help you avoid as many mistakes as possible. I believe a 1:10 mentor to mentee ratio is ideal.

2. Work Buyers and Sellers

Once you understand how real estate transactions work from a buyer's perspective, you are ready to start working with sellers. This is the next step in your career, because you make more money listing homes (since sellers pay the commission). Most agents will want to transition gradually, because working with buyers gives you immediate income, while you wait for your listings to sell (which can take 30 days to 6 months). Working with buyers is much like working an hourly job: you have to put in a certain amount of time to get paid. Working with sellers allows you to convert a lot more sales in a lot less time, while working from any location. Once you list a home, all the other agents work to bring their buyers to bring about the sale. So continue to work with buyers until you're ready to do listings exclusively. This will enable you to generate consistent income, while still leveraging buyers' agents through your listings.

3. Do Listings Only

Once you've got enough money in reserve, you can move over to doing listings only. On a good team, you'll still have lots of administrative support—a closing coordinator, a marketing person and so on—so all you have to do is list the homes (I'll cover a lot about getting listings in Chapter 3). You will see a shift in how you spend your time, as you will now be able to close more sales in the year than you would be able to working exclusively with buyers, or with a mixture of buyers and sellers.

4. Start Your Own Team

Life as a listings agent is great, but you are still only able to earn income from your own efforts. If you're serious about *Exploding*, you have to look at starting your own team. Of course, it's a little difficult to determine exactly when you should do this. If you jump too early, you could easily go under, but if you wait too long you risk becoming complacent as a team agent. There is no precise way to quantify how much business volume and savings is "enough," but I would say if you're consistently moving three homes a month and you have three months of projected expenses saved, then you should be good to go.

You want to get to this point as quickly as possible, especially if your splits are structured in a way that offers you diminishing returns on your labor. However, don't discount other benefits that the team may have to offer, such as transaction coordination and marketing. These items will now be your responsibility, so you will need to account for their cost in your budget.

During this time you will probably need to develop a niche market. This is not to limit you, but to allow you to develop expertise and build up your client base. The niche market that catapulted me to the top was REO properties. Yours might be too, or it might be helping empty nesters, first time home buyers, military families or investors. Your niche doesn't have to define your company; it's just a way to build up the volume you need to get your company off the ground.

5. Get Listings, Hire and Train

Once you've started your own team, you keep the majority of the commission from each sale, but you also spend all your own money for administrative costs and marketing. As a team leader, there are three main jobs you should be focused on: List, Hire and Train. Generate property listings. Hire buyers agents. Train your agents to close deals and service clients. These are the most dollar productive activities you can do as a team leader. And remember, if you list homes and your agent brings the buyer to the table, you're getting commission on both sides of the deal (some brokerages don't allow this or have special rules for these situations, so be sure to ask).

6. Promote a Listings Agent

As soon as you're doing enough business, you can promote one or two of your buyers' agents to become listings agents. Then you can gradually retire from doing listings and just run your business, which should primarily involve hiring and training at this point. In my opinion, you should always have more buyers' agents than listings agents, because listings generate more buyers. Buyers often need to see multiple houses before they make a decision, which is obviously time-consuming.

7. Become a Broker

At some point, you will generate so much business that it won't make sense for you *not* to open your own brokerage. Just like starting your own team, you will decide if what your broker does for you is worth what you pay him or her. You will also determine if you have the time and desire to assume all of his or her responsibilities. I'll discuss this in Chapter 2, so you know if and when this is right for you.

8. Expand

There are several options for expansion beyond your own single-office brokerage, depending on how far you're motivated to take it. You can simply open multiple offices, which can be done by hiring a managing broker or acquiring an existing office. Don't be afraid to think big. You can open multiple offices in multiple states. Keep in mind you will need to discuss (with your accountant and attorney) qualifications for your company to conduct business across state lines. You can run a franchise or a large corporation. You can even become a publicly traded company. Each of these steps brings in more money, and I'll cover them in detail in Chapter 9.

If any of this sounds intimidating, don't worry. You can stop and park at any step in this process, as long as you're content. You will still be making plenty of money. But for those who are motivated to *Explode*, money management is the key to moving from one step to the next. You can't go from being a listing agent to a team leader if you're running off to Tahiti every other weekend. But I'll cover all that in more detail in Chapter 10.

Crash Course

So how did I get into real estate? Like many little boys, I thought I was going to be a professional baseball player. But when no professional team expressed interest in my services, I followed in my granddad's footsteps and became a union plumber. So my first experience with real estate was as a home buyer.

My realtor really had her work cut out for her. I knew absolutely nothing about home ownership. I couldn't ask my parents, since they had never bought a house, and I had never lived in one. With limited funds, my choices were few and far between, so I had to depend on my agent to educate me.

Still, at the age of nineteen, I moved out of my apartment and into a home. It felt like a huge milestone in my ability to make the life I wanted. It was also my first lesson in credit, as I now had more debt than I could pay off in 25 years.

Shortly after we moved in, my wife and I had a baby girl, Shayla. Three quick years later, everything changed. My marriage fell apart, and I became a single father raising Shayla alone. I had to get her out of bed while it was still dark and drop her off at daycare in her pajamas. She was out of the house until I came to get her just before dinner. This was not the life I wanted for her, but I didn't know what else to do. I had been a plumber for five years, and I was moving up in the ranks. Yet I knew I would be out at the crack of dawn every morning unless I did something differently. I just couldn't see my daughter having school plays and other functions without me there.

The idea of real estate came to me when I saw my friend Lonnie arrive at our church softball practice in his latest car: a brand new Cadillac Escalade. He was a team leader for a local brokerage, and the more I thought about it, the more I figured he had to be doing something right.

"Hey, Lonnie," I told him after practice. "I want to get into real estate like you. What should I do?" Lonnie smiled and suppressed a polite chuckle. I was still very rough around the edges, and looking back on it, I can't imagine what was going through his head.

"Sure!" He smiled. "Just take the course and get your license. Then come into the office and we'll talk."

Well, I took the sixty-hour class, while keeping my day job and caring for my daughter. I took the test, passed on my second attempt and showed up in Lonnie's office in my bright orange Nike t-shirt and basketball shorts ready to sell houses. Fortunately, he didn't laugh me out of the room!

First Steps

My plan for real estate was to succeed or die trying. I quit my job, dropped my daughter at school and prayed I would sell a house that month. As it happened, I sold four that month and thirty that year.

The real estate licensing class gives you lots of sobering statistics on how many people try to become agents and end up quitting. In my class, the teacher told us that only two of the thirty people that were there that day would be in business in a year. In two years, there would only be one of us. I never found out exactly where he got his numbers, but my observations over the years agree with what he said. It's a tough business, and the market is often unpredictable and unforgiving.

So why do we do it? Why do we even want to be in this business? Well, for a lot of us, it seems like the perfect job. You're selling the American Dream, you have flexible hours and you get to spend your work day connecting with people. And it really can be a lot of fun, but I learned very quickly that there's a lot more to it. "Flexible hours" can mean working non-stop, especially at first. And while a lot of people want to be real estate agents, many think that just showing up to work means the customers will magically come. But most of us find out sooner or later that it takes a lot more than that.

Looking back on it, I would have never made it that first year if I hadn't started out on the right team. I didn't have to worry about all the extraneous details of running a business, so I began immediately showing homes to clients. I also benefitted from the many years Lonnie had spent cultivating relationships with trustworthy termite inspectors, title companies, attorneys and so on.

By the time my fourth client signed on the dotted line, I was consumed with typical newbie arrogance. "This is so easy!" I thought to myself. Never mind that the deals I had just done were only a tiny fraction of the business that the team as a whole was doing. To me, that commission was all the money in the world. I gained so much confidence from those deals that as far as I was concerned, the sky was the limit. Why wasn't everyone in the office a million-aire by now, I wondered.

Leaving the Nest

Although I found great success as a buyers' agent, from my first month on Lonnie's team, I knew I wasn't going to be there forever. From the very beginning, I was direct with him. "I want to learn to do what you do," I would remind him. And like any good team leader, Lonnie obliged. I asked questions about everything and took note of how everything was done. I read as much as I could about the industry in the evenings, counting the cost of going out on my own. I even used my weeks of experience to critique how Lonnie ran his business! And once again, he was polite enough not to laugh me out of his office.

After Lonnie got his broker's license, the time seemed right. I had been on his team a year, and now I could become a team leader and keep him as my broker. I was loyal, so this is what I felt most comfortable doing. Still, I was nervous. The move would involve taking a huge risk, and the market was just showing signs of being in serious trouble. But I could see myself getting comfortable in the role of a team player if I stayed much longer, so I took the plunge.

Geographically, my move to becoming a team leader was just a different desk across the office. Financially, it meant I was paying commissions on business I had gotten from the old team, while paying all the new fees associated with being the Rhyan Finch Team, which consisted solely of Rhyan Finch!

Once I hired more buyers' agents, I focused on getting listings. This set up the winning situation where agents were making money *for* the team, but they were also making lots of money *because of* the team. I never competed with them, because I was totally focused on making sure their phones were ringing off the hook. We have doubled our business almost every year since I started out, closing 554 properties in 2011 and over 900 in 2012. Despite the fluctuations and downturns in the market, we continued to sell nearly 500 homes in 2013 and 2014 with a team of 20 agents.

As our business continued to grow, I was able to retire from listings and train some of my long term buyers' agents to list homes. I still continued to hire and train. After obtaining my broker's license, I left Re/Max in 2013 with fifteen agents and five support staff members. At this moment, I have 2 offices, 60 agents, and 7 staff people on my team. This has been an incredible journey, and I truly believe we're just getting started. In the chapters that follow, I'll share the lessons I've learned along the way.

Chapter 2:

Turning a Profit

Confidence can be a blessing and a curse. Going out on your own requires a lot of confidence in yourself. And at first it feels awesome: the wind is at your back, and the sky's the limit!

Then you pay your first month's rent and your company fees. And if there's any money left after that, you try to market yourself.

I was a successful team agent, and I was as confident as they come, but I almost didn't make it. Within a few weeks of being out on my own, I wanted nothing more than to go to my broker and beg him to take me back on our old terms. My hope is that this chapter will help you avoid all my mistakes.

Pay Attention to Splits

When you're starting out as a buyers' agent, you must look critically at how you will split your commission with your team leader. My time as a team agent taught me that split incentives often cause an agent's most profitable percentages to fall at the slowest time of the year (the winter holidays). This causes a lot of agents to leave in January when the splits reset.

There are a wide range of split options out there. Some brokerages offer 100% and charge a fee, while others take a percentage with a cap. The best option for you may depend on where you are in your career. Newer agents need to make sure they're getting the support they need in exchange for their splits/fees, while seasoned agents are probably better off keeping the highest percentage of their commission possible to reinvest into business generation. This is even more important when you start your own team, as you will have many more expenses to cover. When I became a team leader, I decided to structure my system so that each month, agents got 40% on their first two deals, 50% on their next two deals and then 60% on every deal after that. For agents who had 12 deals in a 3-month period, the splits increased to 50% for the first two deals each month. This structure enabled my buyers' agents to see higher percentages right away, and it kept my top producers (who do 10-12 deals a month) very happy. This really helped with retention, and it motivated everyone to close deals before the end of the month. That made bookkeeping much easier and ultimately made everyone more productive.

Now that we've been in business for years, my tenured agents are more selective with the deals they do. This enables them to be flexible as the market changes. Although it's tempting as a team leader to offer higher percentages to get agents in the door, it's much better to start with a system you know you can sustain in the long term. Furthermore, the marketing funds and business plan should dictate what you can pay out and still maintain profitability. I rewarded performance by allowing my agents to keep more of their money with our increased volume; they rewarded me by staying loyal and getting it done. And they're still with me today.

Our team model is predicated on the desire to provide real value for the splits we receive. In short what we offer is this:

1st Class Real Estate Independent Agent

- $250 per month brokerage fee

- 95%/5% commission split

- $25 per month each property management asset

- $100 per month fee for any team agent under Independent Agent

- Agent is responsible for all transactions, signs and marketing

1st Class Real Estate Rhyan Finch Real Estate Team Agent

- 40% commission on first two deals each month

- 50% commission on next two deals each month

- 60% commission on 5+ deals each month.

- Team agents are provided with a courier, closing coordinator, receptionist, as well as a listing and marketing coordinator

- Will follow all team guidelines as written in contract

Our splits are more generous than those of most teams and brokerages because we want to motivate good agents to stay with us. We want to offer real value for our splits and fees. We also want everyone in our company to have a balanced life, rather than being so devoted to work that they have no time or energy left for their families and personal lives. Because of this, we have a rotating schedule for our agents so that each one only has to take after-hour calls one night a week.

Death by Overhead

How would you like to work twice as hard for half the money?

That is exactly what my first few months as a team leader were like. Like most of us, I used to dream of that corner office with enormous windows overlooking the city. But in reality, all the perks like that corner office, that mahogany executive desk or any of the other external costs that make a business *look* successful are not worth the peace of mind they rob from you.

But even though I didn't spend lots of money on granite counters and high-end carpet, overhead costs *still* almost put me out of business. If I hadn't grown as quickly as I did, it would have been over.

All agents who consider going out on their own should thoroughly research their office space options before making a move. Doing that would have saved me months of stress and regret. Instead I did the simplest thing: I moved to the other side of my broker's office and paid him rent.

The only thing worse than working all month and not making any money is working all month and *losing* money. The ugly realities of running your own team can be summed up in three words: cost per deal. When I was on a team, the money from each deal went right into my pocket. Now I had to consider my rent, my Re/Max dues, my brokerage fees and my marketing costs. At the time, my rent was $1500. It cost me $495 a month to be an agent, and I paid an additional $495 for each agent I hired. After a few weeks, I realized it was costing me 60% of my previous year's income just to stay open for business! This left nothing for marketing or anything else related to growth (that's why I set up a very different system in my own brokerage that is based on my agents' and my team leaders' success).

Now I run a Profit and Loss analysis of my business every month. Back then I didn't keep track, probably because I didn't want to know. But I would challenge any new team leader to run a P&L every month. You can make it as detailed (including things like paper and gas) or as general as you like, but do it. The sooner you face reality, the sooner you'll figure out what it takes to become profitable.

This will also become a key for helping you to *Explode* in business. I'll explain more later, but for now, download the free app called Checkbook (*https://itunes.apple.com/us/app/checkbook-spending-income/id484000695?mt=8*). Enter and categorize each of your business expenditures, both cash and check, as well as all funds received. If you do this for 30 days, you will automatically have your Profit and Loss records and the budget for each of your major expenses. I know you don't want to do this and don't have the time, but trust me: this is a vital part of the plan for you to *Explode* and have a balanced life.

This strategy has been vital to what I absolutely consider the number one secret of *my* success (besides God): learning to keep my overhead so low that I can be flexible to move wherever the market goes. I will go into more detail in a moment, but for now remember this: corner offices are nice, but staying profitable is even nicer.

Time Limits

One of the unpleasant truths we all confront sooner or later is that there are only 24 hours in a day. I've known motivated and talented entrepreneurs who begin businesses, only to find that they have to work eighteen hour days just to make ends meet. Their gross income may be enough to eek by, but their hourly earnings end up being barely minimum wage, if that.

The same is true in real estate. It's easy to think that if you can just sell a certain number of houses each month, you'll be okay. But I discovered right away that if your price point isn't high enough, your income will be severely limited because there are only so many hours in each day. You may be willing to work as hard as you can, but you *will* run out of time. Those early months out on my own forced me to accept that my work ethic alone wasn't going to make me successful.

Although I'd spent a very profitable year learning the business of real estate, becoming a team leader felt like starting all over again. I was aware before I left Lonnie's team that most of the business I had done had been generated for me. But the reality hit me when I was still splitting commissions on deals I was wrapping up from my role as a team player, while trying to generate new business on my own. Those fees, combined with all my new expenses, had me drowning.

One factor I hadn't considered was the position I'd put my broker in: he had relied on the business I generated, so he needed to make up for the income I would no longer be generating for him. This made it difficult to make the new arrangement a win for both of us. He needed to charge me rent for office space, as well as various fees and splits, to keep his bills paid. Still, our relationship made a difficult arrangement bearable: he was patient with my slow start, and later I was able to renegotiate my deal with him.

Support Staff

When I realized I was working more than twelve hours a day, I knew I had to hire someone. The whole point of going into real estate had been to spend more time with my daughter, and my new endeavor seemed to be defeating that purpose. I made the decision to hire an administrator; I'll call her "Karen." She was a good fit in many ways, and for a brief period, she enabled me to go back to working eight-hour days. The problem with support staff is that they don't generate revenue: I soon realized I had to close even more deals to pay Karen's salary. I was "out on my own," but I was really working for Re/Max, my broker *and* Karen!

I would advise a team leader in a similar situation to hire a virtual assistant part-time, with the awareness that the individual will not be constantly available during office hours. When your Profit and

Loss statements indicate you can comfortably hire a full-time employee, figure out a payroll option and cut the virtual assistant (I was writing personal checks to Karen and dipping into a personal line of equity to survive. That is *not* how you want to do it).

Another lesson I wish I'd understood earlier is that you can double your volume of business without becoming any more profitable. That's because as your business grows, your costs will increase as well. This isn't just office space. Every deal has paperwork that has to be filed. All the money has to be managed and accounted for. If I'd done a better job planning for that kind of growth, I could have avoided some costly mistakes that almost put us out of business.

I finally hired some great buyers' agents, and we got rolling. But because I hadn't planned well, the administrative work began to pile up. We were a sight to see: five of us crammed into a tiny office space, stepping over one another to get to our files. My agents were crushing it in the market, but they were also drowning in paperwork.

We were doing enough business to hire more staff; I just had to get out there and find the right people. I had learned how to be a good agent, how to hire good agents and how to keep good agents. But I still knew very little about how to administrate an office.

Our issue became a crisis when Karen quit. I can see now that she was overloaded, but at the time we were completely unprepared for her departure. I immediately hired a replacement, but she didn't show up to work! I hired a second replacement, and after a week it became obvious that she couldn't handle the job. I had four agents doing an incredible volume of work, but we had no support staff. It was demoralizing for everyone. This is why I always advise team leaders to hire more staff than they need. It will cost you money in the short term, but it's the only way to be prepared for growth and the inevitable ups and downs in peoples' lives. Think of your staff as an army: you want enough members to handle a crisis if needed.

In the midst of this madness, two more agents joined the team. Then I acquired my first twenty REO properties in one day. Now I had six top agents, twenty Fannie Mae properties and we didn't even have anyone answering the phones, let alone preparing files or coordinating closings. We were going to sink if something didn't change fast. That's when we found our saving grace, Emily, who finally replaced Karen and got us back on track.

As far as the long term functionality of our staff goes, my sister Rhendi saved the day in more ways than one. Ironically, we hadn't grown up together, but we'd reconnected as teenagers. It just so happened that she needed a job, but she lived hundreds of miles away in Florida. My desperation and her flexibility led me to hire her as a virtual assistant. She worked for me from home while I hired the rest of the support staff we needed. The crazy thing was she did a better job than any support staff person I'd ever encountered. Her skill and hard work saved the company from catastrophe and set us up for the success we've enjoyed since.

Although she went to school for graphic and web design, Rhendi possessed all the vital qualities of a stellar COO, which is now her title. She is a brilliant multi-tasker. She doesn't just complete her assignments; she thinks them through and has created systems for every process in the office. Now she trains each new support staffer on all our policies and procedures, and I don't have to worry about a thing.

While support staff costs money, its quality can make or break your reputation. Because life happens and some turnover is inevitable, everyone needs a system that can run seamlessly no matter who is manning the desks and the phones. Systems should be so standardized that any competent person could step in if someone leaves or has an emergency.

So learn from my mistakes and set up your systems from the very beginning! Cross train your staff: make sure the receptionist knows how to do the courier's job, and the courier can answer the phones the right way. And if you find someone like Rhendi, hire her and pay her double!

Chapter 3:

Business Generation 101

Hire Producers

My return to twelve-hour days taught me that I needed to hire people who generated revenue, and that meant more agents. I began to ask friends for referrals, but I didn't really know what I was looking for. I knew the basics were important: professional demeanor and good character, so I hired two agents on referrals from friends. On the surface they seemed to be just what we needed; they were kind, polite, great with clients and easy to work with.

Unfortunately, I soon learned they didn't share my drive to succeed. They were similar to the kinds of agents on my old team who were content to do a deal now and then. There's nothing wrong with that mindset, but you pay the same fees on an agent doing one deal a month as you do on an agent who does ten deals a month. Both of them take up the same square footage in your office, but one is producing ten times more revenue for you.

This is where the famous Pareto's Principle comes into effect: 20% of your people will do 80% of the work. If you hire ten decent agents, more often than not, only two will be producers. The trick is to learn what to look for in interviews to find those producers.

There are a ton of different theories on how to find and hire the best. After trial and error, the main quality I look for in an agent is *hunger*. Of all the methods I've researched, I've found that gauging hunger has been the most effective way to determine if someone (who is also reliable and trustworthy) will be a good fit. If people aren't hungry to sell and to grow, there is really no way their goals can line up with yours.

The first hungry agent I hired was Cesar. He was a referral who had seven years more experience than I had, but the downturn in the market had seriously slowed his business. The way I had structured his splits gave him a reason to give my team a shot. The fact that he did thirty deals his first year with me gave him a reason to stay.

The second hungry agent I hired was Amy. She was terrific but had done only four deals the year before she joined our team. Her first year with us, she did thirty! Cesar and Amy showed me that there were hungry agents out there; I just had to find them. Looking back on it, I wasn't lucky to get them; I was persistent.

So after closing only thirty deals my first year on my own, Cesar, Amy and I did sixty deals during our first calendar year together. Then I focused on getting listings and hiring more agents. I hired a third agent who was great but very established and independent. I worked out a slightly different arrangement in her case, which is what I thought I had to do to get her (knowing what I know now, I would caution team leaders not to change their models for anyone). The four of us together closed 120 deals the following year.

The real estate market was crashing, but our business was booming. This freed me up to go after even bigger fish. Our first year together, I had done only listings, and Cesar and Amy had both done both listings and buyers. But soon things grew to the point where I jumped out of doing listings and went after Real Estate Owned properties (REO).

Listings Drive the Industry

The most important lesson of my first year as a team leader was this: listings bring buyers, and buyers bring agents. If you get the listings, the buyers will call. Once you have buyers calling, you can hire the best agents all day long with a clean conscience (because you know you'll keep them busy). Too many brokers and team leaders focus on hiring agents and promising them the world. When the agents show up to work, they soon realize that the broker or team leader just wants to sit back in his office and let them make money for him. They're supposed generate their own leads, and there is no tangible benefit to being on the team.

It's best to approach joining a team like buying a business. You wouldn't buy a business without assessing how profitable it is and whether or not it's postured for growth. Those are the same questions to ask about a real estate team. Lots of the models that worked during the boom don't work anymore. You want to buy into a team with a forward thinking leader and a structure that will enable it to be profitable no matter what happens to the market.

Once I hired more buyers' agents, I focused on getting business. As I mentioned in Chapter 1, this ensured that the team situation was a win for both my agents and for me. Again, I'm not saying you can't have a team leader who is also a buyers' agent, but consider this: if a client who wants to buy a million dollar house walks in the door, it really helps the team to know that the team leader is not going to take that client. He's going to hand the client to one of his agents because he doesn't work with buyers. Instead, he's out there working to get business for them.

Team leaders need to consider what I like to call the 50 X rule when making their schedules for the day (Grant Cardone illustrates this principle well in his book *The 10X Rule)*. Do only the things that bring the team a 50-fold return on the effort: hire an agent that can do fifty deals, find an investor who will buy fifty properties and so on. It's the difference between bringing a bucket of water from the river and digging an irrigation trench. The trench takes a lot longer on the front end, but then the water flows continuously. If you're looking to join a team, seek out a team leader or a broker with patience and persistence to dig the trench. And if you're the leader, start digging!

When a team leader is working hard to keep the agents busy, it's easy for those agents to accept that the commission splits won't change when they generate their own leads. The team leader doesn't compete with the agents, and the agents don't compete with the team leader; everything is predictable and fair. Some months the leader may carry the agents, but other months the agents may carry the team leader.

Short Sales: A Necessary Evil

When the Real Estate market began to crash in 2007, very few people knew much about short sales. Soon, however, it became almost impossible to make it as an agent if you didn't know how to deal with them. Like everyone else, I had to learn on the job. I listed about twenty short sales in a month, and soon that's all I was doing.

I was accustomed to being on a steep learning curve, so I worked all day and studied short sale rules and regulations all night (at least that's what it felt like). As a side note, make sure to do your studying in the evening (8-11pm). You can't close a deal at 11:00 PM, but you can read a book. If you spend your days reading or doing other activities that aren't dollar productive, you have basically missed a day of work. There are a lot of agents who seem busy, but they're put out of business because they don't maximize those daylight hours.

57

Soon, I had listed more short sales than anyone else in my market, but listing them alone wasn't bringing in any money. Then, through painful trial and error, I learned the ins and outs of how to close a short sale and created a system to make short sales work for our team. Through this process, I learned what was (and is) driving the market, why my short sales weren't moving and what to do about it (for those getting started with short sales, Alex Charfan's *Certified Distressed Property Expert Course* is a great resource).

If you'd like to learn the good, the bad and the ugly of short sales, as well as where they may be headed in the future, have a look at Appendix C in the back of this book.

Competing with REO

Let's say you have three agents all listing houses of comparable size and location. Agent A is showing a traditional resale, Agent B is showing a short sale and Agent C is showing an REO. Agent A's sellers are living in their home and have maintained it reasonably well; he lists it for $200,000, knowing the house probably needs $5,000 in new carpet and paint. Agent B's sellers are in deep financial trouble; they've moved out and haven't maintained the home at all. She lists it for $190,000, knowing the house needs at least $10,000 in work to be move-in ready. Agent C's property is owned by the bank. The bank has put $20,000 into it to get a new roof, carpet, paint and upgraded appliances. He lists for $200,000, but then if it doesn't sell right away, he'll drop his price $10,000, or even $20,000. Whose house will sell?

Of course buyers are going to gravitate toward the renovated house that is selling for less. Obviously, the bank is losing money on that house, but that's not the bank's primary concern. Why? Because the person in charge of all the bank-owned properties will repair the home with the expectation that the market will dictate its price. He probably gets bonuses according to how many houses he moves in a given month, and the loss he incurs on an individual property will be averaged with several others when the bank looks at the numbers.

So this is usually what will happen: the bank-owned property sells quickly. The owner of the re-sale doesn't want to lose tens of thousands of dollars on his house, so he either takes his house off the market or sits tight, waiting for the competition to disappear. The problem is that, with 1 in 4 homes in foreclosure, those bank-owned properties keep showing up. And all that time, the short sale just sits there.

So Agent A's time is wasted, Agent B's time is wasted and Agent C makes a killing. When REO's are on the market, they will beat short sales every time. They will be fully renovated, and they will undercut traditional re-sales and short sales. Your only prayer as a short sale agent is to hope that no one gets foreclosed on in the neighborhoods where your short sales are listed.

Poisoning the Well

Imagine you have a tiny vial of toxic waste you need to get rid of, so you sneak out at night and dump it in your town's water supply. Now your immediate problem is solved: you've disposed of your toxic waste, and you've only made the drinking water a little more dangerous. But of course if everyone with a little toxic waste does the same thing as you do, everyone will have big problems.

That's exactly what is happening when realtors listing short sales use common but ill-advised strategies to stay afloat. They list houses for much less than they're worth, and they hold two or three offers on one house. These strategies appear to work in the short term: listing a $200,000 house for $90,000 on the internet *will* generate interest and attract buyers. And holding three offers on one house *will* give the agent a better chance to close with one. But you have to look at the big picture.

That agent holding three offers on one house is keeping three buyers occupied with one house. That means two potential buyers are *not* looking at other houses, and two more homes that should be under contract are still listed as "on the market." The longer those three buyers spend waiting to hear about the house that only one of them will get, the longer there is a perceived over-supply of homes in the area, which drives down prices.

The agent listing a house for well below its worth is attracting buyers, which is what you have to do to stay in business. But ultimately, this survival tactic hurts the market and gives our entire industry a bad name. In some cases, an agent may attract buyers to a home listed for well below market value, only to show them other properties. However, she's also helping to set the expectations of buyers in general. The buyer who saw the $200,000 house listed for $90,000 *will* call. If there are multiple offers on the home, the agent will simply tell him that she's already received a higher offer. Yet that buyer will now think that his best bet is to wait around for the next $200,000 house listed at $90,000 and just make the call faster. His expectations have been set unrealistically low, which will slow down his willingness to make a decision in the future.

Now think about an appraiser looking around a neighborhood to determine the appropriate market price for a house. He won't take into account homes merely *listed* at $90,000, but what if one of them actually sells? Not only has the seller lost money and the agent lost commission, but also everyone in the neighborhood just saw their property values drop by $100,000. So while I understand that agents are trying to do what they need to do to stay in business, we can't poison our own wells in the process.

Lastly, the policy of listing houses which have offers on them as "contingent" instead of "pending" keeps the market artificially flooded. To buyers, it might look as if there are twice as many houses available in their price range as there actually are. And as we should all know by now, an increased supply in proportion to demand will lower prices. All these ill-advised policies and strategies are slowing the recovery of the real estate market and making life harder for all of us.

Reading Economic Indicators

Ultimately, listing REO properties is a great way to thrive as a real estate agent. I've done short sales, I understand how they work and I understand that REO's will beat them every time. But I'm also aware that there are many people who believe that REO's are on the way out. In fact, that's what everyone was saying a couple of years ago when I started selling them. I don't have a crystal ball, but I believe REO's are going to be around for a while, and I'll explain why.

To understand why I don't believe REO's are going anywhere, we have to take a moment and look at the housing market nationwide. During the boom, there were more buyers than houses for sale; housing prices went up, and homes sold quickly. People also bought homes by the skin of their teeth, assuming that if they couldn't pay their mortgage, they could sell quickly, probably at a profit. It was a no-brainer.

Then we had the crash. Lots of people couldn't pay their mortgages and were facing foreclosure.

Add to that the normal number of re-sales that occur because people move, and there were more people selling than buying. Housing prices dropped, putting more homes under water.

We all learned during the boom that you can sell almost anything in a climbing market. After all, if the home your buyer is purchasing for $100,000 is worth $110,000 by the time they close, everybody wins. On the other hand, the longer I worked in short sales, the more it became obvious to me that foreclosures drive down prices in a declining market. Foreclosures lower housing prices, plain and simple. Again, it's just supply and demand: foreclosures put more houses on the market and price them below others of comparable size and location. This seems obvious, but not all agents understand it.

According to a 2011 study by the Cleveland Federal Reserve, properties that were occupied but in foreclosure drove down neighboring property values twice as much as properties that were vacant. During 2012, various states, including California and Nevada, passed legislation slowing or halting foreclosures. In October of 2012, Bank of America halted foreclosures in all fifty states, no matter how many homeowners were behind on their payments. Housing prices began to rise. Fannie Mae and Freddie Mac halted foreclosures in December (as many banks do during the holidays), and the trend continued.

Agents must learn to watch foreclosure rates if they want to understand how to effectively move properties in their markets. As soon as foreclosures slow or stop, it will be much easier to move short sales to both traditional buyers and investors. This leads some agents to believe that short sales are the way to go. But when foreclosures start again, it's get REO or die trying!

The problem, of course, is that even when foreclosures are halted because of legislative action (or the holidays), there is still shadow inventory: houses that aren't being paid for. That dead weight can't sit around forever. In fact, according to *Forbes*, scheduled foreclosure auctions were up 5% at the end of 2014—despite an overall decline in foreclosure rates—mostly due to houses that had been in the foreclosure process for a long time.

Furthermore, it is unclear how long the Mortgage Forgiveness Debt Relief Act will remain law (it was just renewed for another year as of this year, 2015). If and when it expires, we also need to be prepared to have short sales disappear entirely. There will be almost no incentive for sellers to pursue a short sale.

Sometimes banks do offer programs that make short sales more attractive. As of now, Bank of America and Chase Manhattan offer sellers up to $45,000 toward a short sale if their original mortgage is with those banks. Unfortunately, it is almost impossible to know if your seller's loan with Bank of America was actually with Bank of America's money, or if they were merely servicing the loan for Fannie Mae or Freddie Mac. If they were just servicing the loan, then your seller isn't eligible. Bank of America and Chase Manhattan have sent letters to eligible sellers, but unfortunately, most people facing foreclosure aren't opening mail from the bank.

There is another catch. Not long ago I was at a meeting of industry leaders, and I asked if home-owners would be considered liable for the $45,000 in short sale incentive. No one was able to answer my question.

So short sales have always been a very difficult way to make a living as an agent. And in my opinion, they will continue to be challenging for as long as they exist. That doesn't mean you shouldn't list them; it just means you need to have realistic expectations when you do.

Keeping Investors Happy

All real estate agents should learn to serve investors as well as traditional buyers. They are a terrific niche market, because they are almost always buying or selling. In fact, the right investor can get you four deals on one house: you can help him buy a foreclosure from one of your REO clients, and you can help him sell it to one of your buyers once he's done renovating. The key is to know what they are looking for in different market conditions and to anticipate the market by watching foreclosure patterns.

Years ago, investors would buy foreclosures, fix them up and turn a profit. Then the banks got smart and fixed up some of the properties themselves so they could get some of that profit. This undercut investors and drove them to buy HUD foreclosures, since HUD never renovates anything.

It's also important to remember that not all investors are house flippers who want to renovate the homes themselves and then sell. Some may be purchasing properties to rent out. Still others may be managing hedge funds and buying multiple properties as part of a larger financial portfolio.

In fact, hedge funds are becoming a huge part of the real estate industry; their volume of business is large enough to drive prices up or down, depending on whether they're buying or selling. In addition, changes to mortgage laws are making it more difficult for smaller investors to purchase multiple homes as easily as they have in the past, so it's very important to understand how hedge funds work and become the go-to person for managers who want to buy in your area.

To keep your investor clients happy, you need to understand what they need in different kinds of markets. Typically, when foreclosures begin, REO's will not be far behind. This will prompt investors to buy HUD homes or other properties that banks choose not to renovate. The investors will not be interested in selling, because (unless a property is distressed) no one wants to sell in a declining market if it can be avoided. When foreclosures stop, investors are more open to purchase short sales. They are also interested in selling what they have, because prices are rising. This means that by helping your investor clients price their properties correctly, you can build long term, win-win relationships.

The Bottom Line

So what can we expect in the coming years? Do the increasing housing prices in any particular quarter mean that REO's are going the way of the dinosaur and short sales are coming back from the dead? First of all, if REO's truly disappear, it will be because of an authentic recovery in the housing market. That means that there really are more buyers than homes on the market, and those buyers are willing and able to pay more than what those sellers are asking. If that happens, you and I will have other properties to sell and very little to worry about. Then we'll all be doing traditional re-sales, and investors will be making profits.

A temporary recovery driven by artificially halting foreclosures (leaving houses that are under water in the shadows) will not do away with REO's permanently. Sooner or later, the foreclosures have to begin again because banks cannot continue to hold outstanding mortgages forever. And when the foreclosures start, the REO's will be back, and the short sales and re-sales will be undercut and devalued again. If you can stay ahead of these trends, you can learn to thrive in any market.

With that in mind, let's explore how to continue *Exploding* your real estate business with some of my advanced business generation strategies.

Chapter 4:

Business Generation 202

Who is the number one agent in your market? Is it the guy with the huge billboards or the lady with her face in every newspaper? It might be, but if you actually look it up, you'd be surprised how many times the number one agent in a given market is an agent who does little promotion marketing. He probably isn't famous because he doesn't want you coming after his business. Like most guys who have made it to the top, he most likely no longer lists all his properties in the MLS under his name; he's just quietly and steadily selling houses while everyone else struggles.

So unless your territory is in Hollywood or Manhattan, REO's are a good bet. This was the niche market that enabled me to rise to the top in just two years. It allowed me to recruit an incredible team of great agents who are still with me today. And most of all, it opened my eyes to what was really possible in real estate. After selling 900 REO properties, I realized I had been thinking *way too small*.

Of course, I had to learn REO the hard way: trial and error. But now I'm grateful not only to have built a thriving, flexible business of my own, but also to have helped others learn from my mistakes. My goal is to help you learn from my mistakes too.

For Any Doubters

We've talked about why REO's beat short sales and why REO's have slowed down at least for now. But don't forget about the shadow inventory. What is shadow inventory? Essentially it is properties that are in foreclosure, haven't sold or homes that are waiting to be put on the market once prices are more favorable. As of today, Standard and Poor's estimates that we have at least 46 months of shadow inventory lurking behind temporarily rising prices.[1] Those homes won't just go away all by themselves. Sooner or later, banks will have to start foreclosing again.

A few years ago, Fannie Mae and Freddie Mac would hold onto the foreclosures and hire asset managers to coordinate the renovation and sale of the properties. Now that there are fewer houses in foreclosure, they have mostly done away with asset managers. Instead they manage some REO properties themselves (or with a few companies they've hired), and they are bundling and selling the notes of delinquency to investors (as of now, they are losing a lot of money by selling them too low, but this will correct in time). What those investors do with the bundled debt they have purchased will dictate what

---

[1] *http://www.dsnews.com/articles/shadow-inventory-update-46-months-to-clear-supply-of-distressed-homes-2012-05-14*

is coming next for the rest of us. **So follow the money.**

There's also plenty of evidence that the market will encounter another decline, which will put more houses under water. Currently, hedge fund managers are holding several billion dollars in real estate investments, and they keep buying more. Typically, they view these investments strictly from a "spreadsheet mentality," looking only at profits and losses instead of the more nuanced point of view of an experienced local agent. That means that they are likely to dump their holdings at the first sign of trouble, further flooding the market with cheaper homes that have to move fast.

The REO market *does* require work, both to get your foot in the door as an approved agent and to perform as an agent successfully over time. And it requires some money, too (I have found each REO will cost an agent about $1000 to maintain). However, if done correctly, the return on your labor will be better than almost any other real estate opportunity out there.

Remember, when you're doing traditional re-sales, you still have to spend money to generate business. But as an REO agent, particularly for a heavy hitter like Fannie or Freddie, once you close one property, there is typically another one waiting in the wings. This allows you to be more confident when spending money to maintain your REO's because you know that the money will return to you soon. You can also hire based on how much inventory you have instead of how much volume you're hoping for.

So while it may take five or six tries to become an approved REO agent, you can reap the benefits into the indefinite future. Instead of constantly working to generate new leads, you do the work to get their business one time, and then every time you sell (as long as you keep your performance aligned with their standards) your client unloads more houses on you. Instead of chasing more retail listings while your agents close what you have, you just have to make sure your business is running smoothly. To learn more about how to become an approved REO

Agent, see Appendix A. For a detailed explanation of how to successfully manage properties for Fannie Mae, see Appendix B.

But even if you haven't gotten in with a large REO client yet, you can still find investors who purchase REO properties and have them listed with you. If you bring the buyer, that's at least two deals right there.

Remember how I said I closed only about 10% of my short sale inventory each month? Well, that's the national average. So if you list 10 short sales, you can expect to close one per month. With traditional re-sales in a favorable market, you should close 3 each month for every 10 you have listed. REO's? You should close between 5 and 8 a month for every 10 you have listed. There may not be as many REO's as there once were, but they will still be the easiest to move.

The bottom line is this: REO's do require you to invest a lot of work and some money, but it is an investment with an almost unlimited potential for return. That still isn't for everyone: if you just want to make six figures, stick to being a team agent on a good team. There's nothing wrong with that. If you want to make seven figures, start a team, go after investors, get an REO account and add it to your portfolio.

To maximize the potential of REO properties, you must own the market by obtaining a lot of listings. You cannot do this without hiring enough agents! You need agents to answer the buyer calls and to get the listings. This doesn't have to be hard: just focus on the target that gets you to your goal.

Pursuing the Gatekeepers

If you've been in Real Estate for very long, you know that success is not just about what you know, it's about who you know. Nowhere is this truer than in the REO market. Every bank has gatekeepers for its REO properties: the asset managers (who handle the day-to-day sales operations) or sales representatives in your territory. Some may only have vendor managers (who are in charge of hiring the brokers). As an aspiring REO agent, you need to be able to identify those individuals and cultivate relationships with them.

You also want to make sure you're pursuing the right accounts. Unfortunately, some individuals who become approved REO agents only get handed one or two properties. Take the time to investigate which potential REO accounts have the most inventory and pursue them. I pursued the decision-makers at Fannie Mae for about a year before they let me in. I was struggling in short sales and calling, emailing and basically begging to be given a shot. Knowing what I know now, the process could have moved much faster. But it was still unquestionably worth every hour I put in.

I realize that some people find this process very intimidating. I will be the first to tell you that this isn't for someone who can't handle rejection. But believe me, if a former plumber can succeed at it, so can you. I've been told "no" a million times in my life, but I simply never let that stop me.

Rejection is rarely personal, so you never have to take it personally. Just look at it as a test of your desire to do more business. After the Seattle Seahawks won Super Bowl XLVIII, quarterback Russell Wilson shared with reporters something he had said to his team at the beginning of the season. He had pointed out to his teammates that that someone has to win Super Bowl and had asked them, "Why not us?" Someone is going to get those REO accounts: why not you? And like Russell Wilson, you'll need a great team behind you to get it done.

As you connect with the gatekeepers of the banks, you must be sure you are fluent in the vocabulary of the REO world. Most importantly, you must be able to effectively communicate to the gatekeeper that you possess the judgment and decision making skill to get the job done. REO agents do not spend their days sitting down with families around kitchen tables. They are highly specialized professionals brought in to stop the bleeding on a very important patient: the bank. They work in a high pressure corporate environment that cares only about the bottom line; you must convince the gatekeeper that you are up to the task.

And like everything else in life, it's all about following up. Remember that you're not trying to convince the bank that you're the biggest name in your market. You're trying to convince them that you are capable of assessing their properties correctly, keeping them secure, marketing them effectively and moving them efficiently. In short, you are the agent that can help them achieve their goals.

Straight to the Top

After a year of being a team agent and another year of struggling in short sales, becoming an REO agent shot my business straight to the top. My big break came about a month and a half after Fannie Mae brought me on, when an agent in my market (who seemed perfectly good to me) was terminated for performance. Her sales representative handed me 22 listings in one day. I was actually out of town at the time and had to coordinate the transition over the phone. Three months later, we had 150 assets in our portfolio!

Everything changed overnight. Obviously, no one can do 22 BPO's in one day; in fact, I had never done a BPO by myself. So Cesar and Amy were out there, learning right along with me. This gave me a crash course in working *on* my business, not *in* my business. I still reviewed every single BPO that went out, but I had to train my agents and hire more too. There simply weren't enough hours in the day to do everything: the properties were coming too fast.

I was also extremely blessed to work closely with two masters at the game. Jonathan was an agent with multiple offices who had been doing it for years, and he alerted me to how asset managers measured our performance. Leo was a consultant who went around the country training agents in REO management. I listened to everything they said and restructured my business to assess REO's, secure and renovate them as needed, convert listings and close quickly.

Within a few months, I had gone from being on the outside of the REO world to being asked by my supervisors for referrals for more agents. I had gone from being an inexperienced agent desperate to be given a chance to being able to help others. It was an amazing turn of events, to say the least!

Go for the Gold

Getting your foot in the door with an asset manager is more or less the same process, regardless of the bank. But as you can imagine, becoming an REO agent for a small local bank is not going to generate the same volume of business for you as becoming an REO agent for Fannie Mae, Freddie Mac or HUD. I counsel all my agents to go for the heavy hitters. After all, why not pursue the client that can help you sell 50 houses a year instead of the one that can only help you sell 5?

There aren't many heavy hitters, but they have plenty of assets between them. Fannie and Freddie typically handle their own accounts, while HUD outsources through a couple of agencies like Matt Martin Real Estate Services (*http://www.mmrem.com/*) and Ofori REO (*http://www.oforireo.com/*). Vendor Resource Management (VRM) recently took over all the foreclosed homes that had been bought with VA loans. Right now, these accounts will give the right agent multiple properties.

REO isn't the only way to make it big in real estate, but it can be a great way to *Explode* your business. There are advantages and disadvantages with every client. I would advise you not to worry too much about the disadvantages; just get the account and get those listings!

Like almost every aspiring REO agent, I saw the Fannie Mae account as the crown jewel. When I landed it, I knew I had just a month or two to prove myself. As it happened, I ended up moving so many properties that soon I was able to help other agents find the same success by using the same system (For more details on the REO process go to *http://rhyanfinch.com*).

Stories of Success

After I'd been selling Fannie Mae properties for about a year, I got my first opportunity to help someone else do the same. I had him submit his application and then call the decision maker directly. He knew exactly what questions to expect and exactly how to answer them. He was able to effectively communicate his knowledge of the REO process and his detailed understanding of the sales territory. And instead of waiting around for two years, he had about 20 Fannie Mae properties in his portfolio within four months of being accepted.

Part of me couldn't believe the process that had seemed so impossible and mysterious to me had moved so smoothly for the agents I helped. But it was a great feeling, so soon I started helping others. My next client, whom I'll call "Jack," was accepted almost immediately. Jack's office had more agents and was doing a larger volume than my first client. Within four months, Jack had over 80 Fannie Mae properties in his portfolio. Both were doing a great job, saving Fannie Mae and the taxpayers millions of dollars.

It seemed like I couldn't help clients open offices fast enough; soon, we had 20 offices in 8 states! After some internal changes at Fannie Mae, agents like me actually found ourselves explaining to the sales representatives how to get the offices open. Coaching people through the process was becoming a full-time job: before long, I had to hire a new person just to help me screen coaching applicants! While I no longer coach clients through this process, agents that work with me through 1st Class get to take full advantage of my experience. To learn more about being with 1st Class Real Estate anywhere in the country, visit our website at *http://www.1stclassre.com.*

At the end of the day, this was about so much more than making money. We were screening and training people to help a huge government-backed agency mitigate loss to taxpayers. Our experience helped us filter out the people who lacked the work ethic and skills to handle accounts effectively. We were able to identify brokers who would do the best job and have the largest positive impact. The results spoke for themselves: our offices were setting territory records and saving taxpayers millions of dollars.

Making REO work for you

The day I got 22 Fannie Mae properties at once was the day I realized my systems were insufficient to take advantage of the opportunity. I was under-staffed, and I was really just beginning to grasp how much business was actually out there. Fortunately, I realized the gravity of the situation: I knew that I was either going to make this work, or they would never give me another property again.

So I learned as I went. I worked the business and hired staff during the day and learned everything I possibly could at night. And in the end our team made it work. What I know now is that even the most brilliant multi-tasker on the planet can't man-age all the details that an REO client like Fannie Mae requires. You simply can't do it.

Remember, all REO's require a lot of tasks that regular re-sales don't. To name just a few: you have to get your BPO's done on time. You have to confirm the listing price with your sales representative and figure out how you're going to deal with it. Depending on the state of the property, you need to get repairs and renovations approved and then make sure they get done on time. Then you have to monitor every offer and counter offer that comes in so you can get that property sold.

You will need an army to get all this work done on multiple properties over a 10,000 square mile territory, and it has to be an army of competent, effective individuals. But you also have to oversee everything that's going on. You may eventually hire an individual that you can trust to review a BPO to make sure it was done correctly, but chances are you will need to personally review everything of consequence for a very long time.

This is why the quality of your systems is absolutely vital. To be a successful REO agent, especially for Fannie Mae, you must be the one driving the process. You do not want your sales representative calling you; you want to be calling him because your system keeps you on top of everything.

The great part is that once you set up a good system, the bank will want to load you up with as many properties as your team can handle. Banks with REO properties are almost always interested in performance. No matter how many approved REO agents they have, they'll give the properties to the agent who they know can get the job done. And if foreclosures stop and REO's are in shorter supply, that system will still be more than sufficient for moving short sales or traditional re-sales.

I learned a great deal working with Fannie Mae, and our team did an incredible volume of business. But far more important than the volume we did or the money we made was the fact that we perfected our systems in the process. Then when we were no longer with Fannie Mae, we didn't miss a beat. We were set up to take advantage of the other incredible opportunities that were out there (I'll discuss systems in great detail in chapter 9).

In order for you to *Explode* your business while keeping a balanced life, you'll need to cultivate a culture that values both performance and relationships. This will be the difference between a life of freedom and a life chained to your business. In the next chapter, I'll explain how to do this.

Chapter 5:

Training

Setting up a System

To do anything successfully over the long term, you have to have a system that enables you to repeatedly generate the results you want. Being so new to real estate and the business world in general, I wasn't even entirely sure which questions to ask a new client. Forgetting to ask for an important piece of information meant I had to call back. If I didn't reach them right away, the process got bogged down.

Learning to be as efficient as possible was the way to avoid working eighty hours a week. This meant automating as many parts of the process as possible. Before long, I had created a list of all the questions to ask the clients who called to get a price on a house. It is the same list my team and I use today:

1. ***How long have you been looking?***

2. ***Do you have an agent?***

If buyers already have representation, give them the information they need and move on. (This is the law in Virginia.) If they don't, the game is on!

3. ***Have you been pre-approved?***

If buyers haven't been pre-approved, put them in touch with a trustworthy loan officer who can take care of it.

4. ***What is your phone number, email and address so I can send you some information?***

This ensures you can contact them when you need to.

5. ***When is a good time to get together to go over what you are looking for?***

Make sure to end each call (with an unattached buyer) with an appointment to meet. In fact, the whole point of the conversation is to get to this fifth question and turn your phone call into an appointment.

This simple system made me more efficient and greatly increased the number of calls I was able to convert into appointments. It also increased the number of calls I was able to make because I didn't waste time with a bunch of unnecessary questions. Lots of agents think they need to spend a lot of time on the phone in order to effectively connect with the client. In fact, it's a much better use of your time to make your questions count, connect quickly and move on to call the next person.

I also developed a packet of information very similar to what my second real estate agent had handed me. I knew from experience that all good agents go out of their way to educate buyers. All of this probably sounds basic to an experienced agent, but for me it was brand new. And some agents who have been in the game a long time still haven't perfected their systems, or they make them too complicated to work well. This creates lots of unnecessary

94

work and slows down the entire process. Within weeks, I saw that the more efficient my system was, the more deals I would be able to close without compromising the quality of service. To learn how we educate our clients and to get a complimentary copy of our buyers' packet visit *http://rhyanfinch.com*

The Training Myth

Some real estate companies brag that they will train you (for free, of course) to be the perfect agent. On the surface, this promise seems great. You go to a week-long seminar where you learn everything from how to write the perfect contract to how to or-chestrate the perfect closing. Then you may get a week or two to shadow other realtors and learn how your new office runs.

The problem is this: at the end of your month of "training," you have made no money. And you'll soon learn that every deal is different anyway, so you still haven't been perfectly prepared for every detail you will encounter in the future. It's one thing to know how to write a contract; it's another to know how to solve the problems that come up so you can close the deal. So that "free" training just cost you a month's salary!

Agents like Cesar and Amy were experienced. All I had to do was explain our system and turn them loose on the buyers. When we do get inexperienced agents (who are hungry, of course!), I tell them that they will learn by doing. While it might seem like I am throwing them to the wolves, I know that they will learn more by actually doing deals and asking questions along the way than they will from sitting in a seminar going broke.

Of course all our new agents are assigned to a mentor agent, who is compensated for being available to answer their questions and to help them along the way. I have concluded that truly hungry agents would rather be making money while they learn than be trapped in a room listening to someone tell them how to make money. Our on-the-job training philosophy is another way we attract and keep top agents.

That said, we do have continual training for everyone, and we have very tight quality control. A report is drawn up on every deal and sent to me to review personally, and every phone call we make or receive is recorded. I train with my team every other week, and on the alternate weeks I train team leaders in my other offices. These are not just motivational meetings; they are detailed strategy sessions, which equip all our agents and teams to be as productive as possible.

As you hire new agents, you must ensure they are properly trained in your system and standards. Ongoing training is absolutely vital to growing your business. You cannot compromise quality of service, so you must err on the side of training too much rather than leaving anything up to chance.

Develop your systems and document them with the assumption that you are explaining them to five-year-olds. Omit no detail, no matter how seemingly insignificant. This is not because you want to be condescending or hyper-controlling, but because you want to leave as little room for error as possible.

It is impossible to monitor every single detail of your business; there simply aren't enough hours in the day. So the best way to gauge the quality of work being done is to spot check everything. For example, if you have twenty properties that were supposed to have renovations beginning on Monday, drive by four of them and make sure the work has begun. Record every phone call your buyers' agents are making, but only listen to 10% of the recordings. Develop a way to spot check every system and every employee, and you will have a good snapshot of how everything is running on a day-to-day basis. Then you will know what specifics you need to address in training.

Culture is Key

As your business grows, you need to make sure to invest in your personal growth as a leader. Most people do this by reading books and attending conferences. I had the opportunity to meet Cameron Herold, the author of the book *Double Double: How to Double your Revenue and Profit in Three Years or*

Less. I met him at a time when I was just beginning to live out the book's premise: I had actually doubled my volume each year for three years in a row.

On the surface, everything was going great for me. I was checking off items on my list of goals one by one. I had learned to recruit quality people and had created an incentive system that retained them. I was devoting myself to getting those listings to make sure that everyone stayed busy. My next goal was to be the number one Re/Max team in the state of Virginia.

But reading *Double Double* and speaking with Cameron alerted me to another issue lurking just beneath the surface. In the midst of our growth, I had neglected the culture of our office. The more money we made, the more arrogant and temperamental I became. I would snap at anyone who got something wrong. I was working nearly around the clock, and I expected my employees to do the same. I was quickly developing a reputation for being a difficult and demanding boss.

So I asked myself the question we now ask ourselves in our office all the time: **"Is this the person I want to be, and is this the kind of company we wanted to build?"** The answer at the time was, "No." I wanted my people to *want* to come to work. Sure, I needed them to work hard, but I didn't want them to start resenting their jobs in the process. The whole reason I had gone into real estate was to spend more time with my daughter, and once again, I was losing sight of that goal.

So I made some changes. I called a meeting and informed everyone that I no longer expected anyone to work on Sundays. I told them that I was going to spend that day at church and with my family, and I wanted to give them the opportunity to do the same.

In his book *Developing the Leaders Around You: How to Help Others Reach Their Full Potential,* author John Maxwell notes that the best leaders won't produce followers; they will produce more leaders. I started asking myself what I was doing to help my staff and agents reach their full potentials and started paying attention to their goals and interests outside of work.

One employee confided in me that he was a huge football fan but had never been to a professional game. I was able to get him tickets and passes to meet his favorite players. Another employee wanted to lose weight. I told her to pick out a treadmill, and I had it delivered to her home. There are many relatively low-cost gestures that can show your team that you care about them as people, not just as employees.

Winners want to get paid, but winners also want to be part of a functional work culture that affirms them rather than beats them down. These changes made work a more pleasant place to be. Our new way of doing things meant that the hours we spent together each day were energizing instead of draining, at least most of the time. And the month I decided we weren't working Sundays anymore, we were named Re/Max's number one team in the state of Virginia.

Chapter 6:

Money Management

After enjoying a measure of success in real estate, I had a conversation with my friend Chris that changed the way I looked at money forever. We were enjoying an afternoon out on the water, when our boat passed a beautiful waterfront mansion.

"Hey, you should buy that house!" I joked.

"No way!" he laughed. "I can't afford it." This surprised me. I knew enough about Chris's financial situation to believe that he could have easily purchased a house like that.

"What do you mean?" I asked. "Sure you could."

Chris went on to explain that he only used half his income for living expenses. Everything else he saved or invested. As a result of this lifestyle, he owned his house and all his vehicles outright and had large savings and investments. He didn't consider the house affordable because he couldn't purchase it outright with half his annual income.

The conversation caused me to evaluate my own way of spending money. I had always considered myself pretty cautious financially, but at the time I was struggling to save just 20% of what I earned. Suddenly, my eyes were opened to what was possible, and I made changes that would help my family become financially free and launch my business to new levels.

Personal Money Management

While personal finances may not seem directly related to succeeding in real estate, most people will manage a business the same way they manage their own money. Furthermore, managing your personal finances well is absolutely vital to living a balanced life and having time for your friends and family. The more debt you have personally, the more you have to work to stay afloat.

I remember a man that I'll call "Carl" who had over 200 agents working under him. He and his wife lived in a condominium and were in the market for a larger home. I was shocked to learn that they were going to have to sell their condo in order to have a down payment for their new home. The new house was going to cost a lot more than their condo in monthly payments, utilities, insurance and so on. Yet even after five years in this condo, Carl hadn't set any of his extra money aside. Now he was in a situation where if those agents didn't produce enough for him, he was in big trouble.

"Oh, I never worry about having a $10,000 credit card balance," another friend used to say. "All I have to do is sell an extra house next month. Nothing to it!" That attitude is so typical of all kinds of high-earning professionals, but it keeps us broke and inflexible. We need to budget our personal finances and our businesses. I sometimes joke with my team members that if they go out and buy a Porsche or a Lamborghini, that's great news for me because they'll have to keep working for me to pay for it! But the truth is I want all my team members growing with me.

If you can't manage your personal finances, you'll most likely struggle to manage the finances of your business. Everyone has different theories about how much you should put into savings, how much you should invest and what kind of investments are best. Are car payments okay, or should you pay cash up front for everything? I'm not a professional financial advisor, so I'm just going to share what I've learned and how I do things for my family.

A savings account is basically a safety net for emergencies. Anyone can be hit by an unexpected situation: a sudden illness, a crisis with a family member or some other emergency that demands our immediate attention and prevents us from working. So I think it is common sense to keep at least three months' worth of expenses in a savings account in case something like that happens.

Other important reasons for short term savings include taxes (this is particularly important for all real estate agents!), a down payment for a house and other investments. But if you have enough in savings for your emergency fund and these other goals, should you continue to fill that account at the expense of paying off other debts?

I believe that after you have enough in savings to cover emergencies, you should pay off your debt with the lowest balance and the highest percentage of interest (you will never find a savings account that offers a rate of return equal to the interest rate of your loan). If you have a $7,000 car loan at 8% interest and a $10,000 loan at 3% interest, then you are going to want to pay off your $7,000 car loan faster, since it is costing you more to borrow that money. Once it's paid off, you can use that payment to add to the payment of the next smallest loan with the next highest interest rate.

In general, I would prioritize getting rid of higher interest debt over saving for longer term investments. Interest rates can be front end loaded, which means that the payment you are making every month is going almost entirely to interest, while barely making a dent in your principal. Paying down your principal faster on an 8% loan means you'll "earn" 8% on the debt you paid off, and it's hard to find an investment that guarantees that rate of return.

I believe the smartest way to manage money is to pay off all your debts as quickly as possible, especially on depreciating assets. After all, every month you pay on a car loan, you are paying interest on an item that actually is decreasing in value. If your car loan has a high enough interest rate, you may even consider paying it off before you pay your taxes. The IRS charges you 3% interest (2% for a business), which is probably much lower than what you are paying for your car loan.

Once you're out of debt, don't take on any new debt unless it's an appreciating asset. Start thinking of it this way: if you can't pay cash for a depreciating asset, maybe you can't afford it. You are losing a lot more money than you realize in the long run.

Investing in Financial Freedom

If you were to talk to ten different financial experts about the best places to invest your money, chances are high that you'll get ten different answers. I'm not an economist or a financial planner, but I know enough to realize that you can't just put all your money in a savings account and let the bank have all the fun. So while no one agrees on the best way to grow your money, I'll just tell you what I do with mine.

As my team began working with REO properties, I began to realize how much potential there was in that industry. After all, if I could help my clients make and/or save so much money by assisting with these transactions, why not put my own money to work the same way?

So I started buying houses and flipping them, using the same knowledge I'd used to flip houses for REO clients. But I only bought houses with cash. Most people get into trouble with speculative home buying because they over-leverage themselves.

They're determined to flip as many houses as they can as quickly as possible, so they borrow money up to their ears. If one little thing goes wrong, the entire operation comes crashing down.

For example, lots of people were making money hand over fist when the real estate market was growing. Borrowing money wasn't a problem, and houses were easy to move at a profit. The problem came when the market crashed. Not only were properties harder to sell for the price the investors had been hoping for, those investors were often paying 12% interest on the money they had used to buy their properties in the first place. So every day they couldn't sell, the properties were hemorrhaging money. A temporary downturn in the market became a catastrophe.

If you buy only what you can purchase with cash, you protect yourself from that kind of disaster. First of all, if you make a mistake with cash, you'll just lose some money, as opposed to jeopardizing your collateral or your credit. Second, we all tend to be more careful with cash than with money that the bank is lending us. Third, if you only work with cash, the way you make more money is to flip your properties faster. You don't buy a new house to renovate until you've moved the last one. Flipping quickly at a lower risk (instead of flipping large volume at a higher risk) puts your focus and effort in the place that will give you the largest rate of return on your money.

There are other ways to make money in real estate besides house-flipping. Rental properties can also offer a very good return on your money, especially if you buy them with cash. For example, if you purchase a home for $100,000, pay $10,000 for improvements and then rent it out for $1,100 a month, you are getting a 1% return on your money each month. How many other investments offer you a reliable 12% return a year? Even if you have to deal with non-payments or reinvest some of your profit for maintenance, the risks are still much lower than most other investments.

Another advantage to working with cash in the rental market is that you can get a line of equity against the home that you own outright and use this to buy another property. Then you can essentially collect rent on two properties for the same $100,000, all without paying a fortune in interest. If the houses increase in value, you've made even more money.

Of course real estate investment involves a certain degree of risk; however, so does letting your money sit in the bank. I explained this to my daughter Shayla once when she was going through a pile of quarters in my car. We started playing a game to see if she could guess the year each of the quarters had been minted. Then I explained that the government continues to print and mint more money than it takes out of circulation. This means that over time our money will lose purchasing power, since it's not backed by gold or anything else. The inevitability of inflation means that the money in your savings account is losing value if you don't do anything else with it. The person who lives the dream is not the person who makes the most money; it's the person who manages the money the right way.

It goes without saying that I use my own agents and my own company for these transactions, so I'm saving all the way around. I'm not telling everyone to invest the way I do. I'm just sharing what I do with all that extra money I set aside. There is so much more money to be made in real estate beyond just earning commissions off transactions. There are no guarantees in life, but if you've spent your career studying the housing market, why not get in the game yourself?

Using your money the right way can eliminate a lot of strain on you, your team and your family. Borrowing money tends to add stress and can sap your creative energy. Use the money you make from real estate to buy assets instead of digging yourself more deeply into debt. Be careful with leverage. If your tenant doesn't pay, you have no income from your rental property investment until you can get another tenant. This is why you determine how much to risk based on how much money you have in savings. Your savings account will also afford you opportunities to invest when the right opportunity arises.

Reading the Signs

Working in real estate with the goal of becoming financially free requires knowing more about your industry than the average agent bothers to learn. Doctors study advancements in disease research and treatments, farmers study weather patterns and real estate agents need to pay attention to markets and financial trends. It might sound really basic, but everything that happens in the market has a cause. We're never going to be able to predict perfectly which causes will produce the greatest effects, but the better we understand these causes, the more effectively we can anticipate what the market will do.

A good real estate agent will spend at least a few hours a week reading financial news related to bond markets, interest rates, other industry trends and what the big players like Fannie and Freddie are up to. I have a simple method for reading industry signs. I read DS News (Default Servicing News) every morning. Then I try to figure out what the market will do based on what I have read. If I'm right a couple of times, I'll start to make decisions for my business based on those impressions.

Watching trends and paying attention to how they affect the market helps us know what to do in both the short term and the long term, as agents and as investors. For example, several years ago it was normal for the average family to move every 3-5 years. As a local agent, you could expect a steady stream of referrals based on that rate. But when those behavior patterns change, it affects not only the number of transactions in an average neighborhood but also the number of referrals you can expect to receive. It's also a good idea to attend local business events when you can. These not only help you network with other professionals but also give you a sense of what is going on in your local economy.

At the end of the day, selling real estate is a job just like anything else. As long as you have to go back to work and sell another house, you're stuck.

And no matter what profession you're in, you have to save enough cash to invest for the future.

Real estate is also demanding. Whether you are a team agent, out on your own or running your own brokerage, you can get sucked into working around the clock if you're not careful. Making smart personal spending and savings decisions, while continuing to educate yourself financially, will allow you not to be pulled into the rat race. Furthermore, business and financial success will never bring us the satisfaction and peace that healthy, loving relationships will. And for most of us, that means finding a way to prioritize our families in the midst of the craziness. Remember, money doesn't mean anything if you can't enjoy it with the people you love most.

Chapter 7:

Making It Work

Most people in the Hampton Roads area know me as Chantel's husband. She is an incredible leader and known for being number the number one real estate team in our market. In this chapter, I'm going to talk about how we balance our home and work life and how you can do the same. Because, as you'll see, **I believe the health of your business is directly related to the health of your relationships**.

Inspired to be Better

Even though Chantel and I enjoyed our first date, I'm pretty sure she never intended to go out with me again. She was the queen of our market, and I just seemed like a young amateur in comparison. But she had let it slip out during dinner she was a diehard Redskins fan. And even though I hate the Skins, I bought tickets to the biggest game of the season against the Cowboys and invited her to go. What could she say?

After a year of dating, we got married. She was better than I was at almost everything. She had a phenomenal personality, a killer work ethic and an incredibly strong brand. While I rarely attended networking events, she went all the time: she knew everyone, and everyone knew her.

It's very easy for men to feel threatened by a woman's success, but I had to deal with it or be miserable. I learned that ultimately—if you're going to have any healthy relationships—you have to be inspired by the success of others, not threatened by it. Being Chantel's husband didn't make me feel less successful. It challenged me to be better.

Most of the time, if a husband and wife both work in real estate, they work together. Chantel and I happen to be competitors, but we've found that competition doesn't have to be an ugly thing. Of course we would never undermine one another, but we would never intentionally undermine any other competitor either. After all, real success comes from improving yourself, not tearing anyone else down.

There are also advantages for us working for different companies. When people ask me why we don't join our businesses, I often joke that Chantel is the boss at home, so I don't want her to be my boss at work too! But in reality, we are both strong leaders with strong personalities. We use different business models and have slightly different management philosophies. Our businesses give us each a healthy outlet for our leadership abilities and reduce our tendency to boss each other around at home.

To have a thriving family and a thriving business, you need to make sure you are investing the same effort into both. The same character qualities that make you a good leader at work will make you a good spouse and parent. Real leaders serve, and Chantel and I have learned to serve one another. Real leaders think ahead, and we've learned to plan for the needs and activities of our household with the same care and forethought we use at work.

All About Efficiency

If the structure of your business isn't sound enough for you to spend quality time with your family, it isn't sound enough to grow. If you're working around the clock to make everything function, how can you possibly increase your volume? Ultimately, the same qualities that allow you to grow a business will allow you to balance your work and your relationships.

Both relationships and business demand time, and there's only so much time in a day. However, if both Mom and Dad quit their jobs to spend all day with their children, it would not make them better parents. They would not be teaching their children a good work ethic, and there would be no money to pay the bills. In the same way, giving all your time to your business and letting your family time slide will not make your business successful in the long run. Working late nights is often a substitute for developing sound systems and structures that will eventually free you to do other things. If you don't have enough time for your family, I can promise you your business will ultimately end up dysfunctional.

At this point in my life, I am at the office running 10 companies between 9:30 am and 4:00 pm. I could probably make more money if I stayed later, but at some point you have to ask yourself, "How much is enough?"

John D. Rockefeller's answer was supposedly, "One more dollar." But there's a difference between being driven to be the best that you can be and valuing money above relationships. Financial success means nothing if you sacrifice your family along the way.

When it comes down to it, it's not the income I make today; it's what I did with the income from yesterday and the time from the day before. This is why I have harped on the management of time and money so much throughout this book. If you want to work 24/7 and make all the money you can, then that's okay too. Just understand you may miss out on the other parts of life. I'd challenge yourself to come up with a way to get the same income you want, while structuring your time better so you have more freedom and balance.

Of course there may be seasons when you have to put in 12 hour days to get a business off the ground or to another level. I certainly had to do that at times. And if you're spending 12 hours a day doing dollar productive work, in time you'll be able to hire others and get back to a better schedule. But if you're stuck in a long-term pattern where you're working all the time and neglecting your relationships, it's a sure sign your business is not running efficiently. That means it's time to put more effort into working *on* the business instead of *in* the business.

There is a huge difference between working hard and being productive. Being efficient means you can produce great output with less input of time and energy. A farmer who harvests his crops by hand works much harder than the one who uses a huge mechanical combine. But the second farmer is far more productive. Unfortunately, too many of us are stuck in inefficient patterns that rob our families of the time they deserve.

A farmer harvesting everything by hand will not be able to handle planting two more fields next year, even if he works from sunrise to sunset. In the same way, there is no way your business will grow if you are doing everything yourself. In business, good systems are the equivalent of the mechanical harvester. They enable you to produce more with less time and energy.

Setting up a sound structure for your business is something that takes time on the front end, but you reap the benefits into the indefinite future. As a leader, your goal isn't just to achieve balance in your own life; you want a company culture that encourages balance for all your employees. We set up a schedule for everything that needs to be done in our office, which ensures not only that all responsibilities are covered, but also that no one is unfairly burdened. Employees with healthy balanced lives will perform better in the long run.

Success is a Choice

Businesses don't succeed by accident, and neither do families. Unfortunately, many people fail to realize that the same qualities that make you a successful business leader can also make you a great spouse and parent. We have to approach both our work and our relationships with a sense of purpose and determination.

I take the goals I set for myself as a father just as seriously as the goals I set for work. As of today, my goal is to spend four uninterrupted hours with my family every day. Last year, I wanted to teach my son to walk and talk and to take my family on a memorable vacation. I wanted to be at my daughter's important school events and to support my wife in all of her personal goals. These are the things that are most important to me, and I work for them just as deliberately as I work for everything we are doing at the office.

Again, I would never say that I do everything perfectly. Like most agents out there, I've answered the phone at the dinner table, and I've gotten on the computer to check on something when I should have just left it alone. But I'm still blessed with close relationships with my kids and my wife because I take the field trips and the anniversaries just as seriously as I take a closing or a business deal.

On a practical note, the sooner you figure out which work-related tasks only you can do, the better it will be for your relationships. We pay our support staff a competitive salary instead of an hourly wage. This allows us to give them additional responsibilities and frees me up in the evenings. Since real estate can be a round the clock endeavor, I have an assistant that can deal with emails and calls between 5:00 PM and 11:00 PM, when I want to be focused on my family. Of course there might be calls I need to deal with, but then the assistant can text me, and I can make that decision, rather than having to answer every single email myself.

If you're struggling to spend time with the most important people in your life, start with a list of everything you do in a week. Which activities generate revenue? Which can be delegated away? Try to focus on activities that only you can do or the activities that generate the most income. If someone else can post your signs or pick up your lockboxes, pay them to do it. And definitely try to cut out the work activities that waste time, whether it's taking certain phone calls, pursuing leads that are unlikely to materialize or attending unnecessary events. This is an important step for growing your business and spending time with your loved ones.

Everyone's office is different, and everyone's family is different. There is no one right or wrong way to balance the hours in the day, and all of us will mess up sometimes. But if we grow healthy businesses and make our families a priority, we can see both thrive.

What's the Point?

Why do we want to be successful? What is the point of financial or business success if our personal relationships suffer? As I've shared repeatedly, my whole reason for getting into real estate was to make a better life for my daughter. When Chantel and I got married and had our son, that dream expanded: I wanted to be the best I could be as a husband, a father and a businessman.

After we'd been married four years, I finally closed more deals than Chantel. Of course she closed all hers in our local market, and I had to set up offices across the country. The funny thing is, as my business has grown, I don't feel any different about myself. Of course it feels great to have people ask for your advice or opinion on something, but honestly most people in our market still know Chantel more than they know me because of the strength of her brand.

But both of us agree, we'd much rather have a healthy balance in our lives than be "number one." Also, the more successful we have become, the more we have resisted putting our names and faces out there for the public to see. This is not just because we want to be able to have a quiet evening out; we don't want to talk about real estate 24 hours a day. Part of having a balance in life means other interests:

it could be tennis, softball or playing in a band. We all need enriching activities outside of work.

Even better, find a cause bigger than yourself and help those who can never repay you. Whether it's homeless ministries or veterans, you can find a charitable endeavor that needs your help. Personally, I'm passionate about helping orphanages. My grandmother and grandfather met in an orphanage, ran away and got married. Seeing how far they have come has taught me that anyone can pursue their dreams, regardless of how things start out. Find what matters to you and make a contribution as an important part of your own legacy.

At the end of the day, work is what we do, it's not who we are. We want our businesses to represent our characters and our high standards of service, but we don't want them to own us. The good news is we *can* have it all. We can't take every phone call, attend every event *and* be at every school play or basketball game, but we can have thriving businesses and thriving families. But if I ever had to pick, I'd choose my family every time.

Chapter 8:

Leverage

My first introduction to leverage was in wrestling. Although I was new to the sport, I was brimming with confidence when my much shorter opponent entered the ring. A few seconds later, I found my face leveraged into the mat, as my opponent successfully pinned me.

That match taught me that size wasn't an advantage unless you learned how to use it properly. The shorter wrestler had used his lower center of gravity and shorter stance to attack my leg from an outside angle. It would be a few weeks before I learned to leverage my height to throw shorter opponents off balance and grab that ankle.

Financial leverage, at its heart, is getting the most out of your money. Just like an actual lever can utilize a relatively small amount of force to lift a very heavy object, learning to leverage your money and time properly enables you to do a lot with a little. But in order to leverage your time and money well, you must move beyond living hand to mouth, making just enough to cover your expenses. This means not only making more money, but it also means spending less. In short, you have to stick to your budget.

This type of leverage is more like a spring. If you want to jump into this career or to the next level of this industry, you need to get low and spring to the next level with all the force you can. Reducing the personal and business spending will allow you to spring forward in your real estate career.

Three Accounts

After I got things together as a team leader, I began running my team with **three accounts: an operating account, a budget account and a savings account.** This is how you can get your money to tell you what to do in your business.

The goal for your operating account is to hold 6 months of your budget account. So if your budget for the month is $5000, your goal is to have $30,000 in your operating account. If you're just starting out and have no money saved up, I suggest going to a team until you're in a financial position to branch out on your own. Stay there until you have at least 3 months of expenses saved after you have paid for all the items you will need to start, like business cards, a website, a lead manager and signs for the yards.

On the first of each month, you take what you need for your month's expenses from your operating account and put it into your budget account. You track this amount closely, so you know what you will need for marketing, overhead, salaries and so on. The budget account is kept lean so that you can't spend money carelessly. If it runs out of money for the month *you can't spend any more*. Trust me, this will save your career if you follow this rule. No excuses!

You may start with a smaller budget. That's okay! But that means you can't buy the leads, *you have to work for them.* This forces you to call leads, do open houses and follow the referral regimen detailed in *The Seven Levels of Communication* by Michael Maher

(*http://www.amazon.com/7L-Levels-Communication-Relationships-Referrals/dp/1940363217*).

Here is where it gets really interesting. You also want to designate a certain percentage of each check that comes in for savings - the minimum is 10% (you can utilize this account for tax money too, but any money for taxes should be on top of the 10%). You are **NEVER** allowed to take money from savings unless it's going to come back with a friend. This means that money from savings is only for expenditures that will bring in revenue, such as buying a rental property, flipping a home or investing in another business. It is NOT for your budget expenses (side note: I strongly recommend having different colored checks for these three accounts to prevent errors and confusion). What if you want to hire a staff person or a get a Trulia account with money from savings, you ask? No! This is strictly for assets, not operating expenses! This is how you get out of having to sell in the long run. Some people call this empire building, but it is the key to your long term financial freedom. So let's look at this with a real scenario.

Suppose you have a check come in for $6000. It comes into your operating account, and it's the only check you got this month. You move $600 to savings right away (10%). You move $4000 to your budget account (this includes a $3000 salary to you). That leaves $1400 in your operating account. The next month goes by, and another $6000 check comes in. Now you have $2800 in your operating account and $1200 in savings. At this rate, you will need to continue for 17 months to get the 6-month reserve ($10,200) so you can raise the limit on your budget account. Keep in mind you should sell more than one home a month. If you're not doing this you need to stay on the team until you're averaging at least 3 deals a month.

Once you have about three months' operating expenses saved, you can start doing listings exclusively. This is a crucial time for your business. You have to list as many properties as you can to get the buyers to call. The more buyers calling, the more you can leverage the work of a growing number of buyers' agents on your team. However, if the monthly fees you pay on your buyers' agents are too high, they will slow your growth. If they are relatively low, you can simply add the volume of the deals they do without worrying about disrupting your budget.

If you don't have the cash to pay for lead-generation (more on this in the next chapter), then you'll have to work to generate leads. Train your agents to do open houses and to utilize social media and other systems to generate referrals. Continue to list, hire and train, and don't violate the rules governing your three bank accounts.

Preparing for Growth

Growing my own business this way—I actually put 50% into savings each month—had several immediate effects. First, I was extremely motivated to generate as much business as I possibly could so that the 50% I spent could be as large as possible. Second, I was able to pay off debts the business had incurred and later pay off the rental homes my other company owned. Third, I was well prepared for tax time when it came around. Fourth, I had cash on hand when new business opportunities arose.

What I learned in the process is that even though I hadn't been spending indulgently before, I was still not positioning my business for optimal, sustainable growth. It's so easy to convince ourselves that we can spend some money this month and make it up next month, but you simply *can't* sustain growth if you are over-leveraged. If you have deep cash reserves, however, the sky is the limit.

Any business (or individual) can have a good month or two, but only those with the discipline to plan for the future will be able to turn good months into good years. I learned the hard way that you can't be understaffed when an opportunity presents itself: I had no support staff and then got handed 22 REO

134

properties in one day. The only reason we made it is because I worked 18-hour days until our staff situation was under control. Now I'm in a position where I don't have to put in more hours to make more money; I just look for a way to get a higher rate of return on my investments.

If you want to posture your company for growth, you need to have more than enough team members so that you can handle an increase in volume without compromising quality of service. To do that, you need to spend *less* on overhead and other optional expenses. We need to be as professional as possible for the least amount of money, not as luxurious as possible for as much as we can spare.

Besides wasting money on overhead, some business leaders make the mistake of delegating tasks away for the purpose of putting their feet up. Truly successful people never get complacent, just like real athletes never stop training. They don't use their spare time to sleep in late or take lots of long weekends. They are constantly learning, growing and preparing for the next opportunity. For me that meant reading more books on real estate and financial management and saving lots of money.

Even this book took shape in my spare time, not during office hours. Right now, it is snowing in Virginia Beach, and schools are closed tomorrow. My family is asleep, and I am in my home office working on the book. While my competition is lying in bed, I'm working on something that will keep working for me when I'm done. That's what you have to do too, if you want to get ahead of the competition.

You never know when the next big door will be opened to you. When it is, you want to be able to handle it at a high standard when no one else can. Think of the cash you have on hand as the wind in the sails of your business: it will determine how far you can go when the next opportunity comes along.

If you're not preparing yourself for growth, you are actually posturing yourself for decline, whether you realize it or not. Let's say you have two bad months. You don't have cash reserves, so you decide to lay off some staff. The next month, your prayers are answered: you are presented with a tremendous opportunity. But you no longer have the capacity to handle it because of the layoffs, which have also lowered morale. You either miss the opportunity, or you take it and try to hire along the way. But the second strategy puts your company at risk for performing at a lower level, which could easily damage your reputation.

Of course there are times when you have to let someone go. Maybe it's due to performance or because a position is no longer necessary. But those are decisions you make based on the needs of your business, not the fact that you had a couple of months where your revenue declined. The bottom line is this: spending more money than you take in will put you in debt. Debt forces you to make more money just to keep up with the bills. But when you make more money, you incur a greater tax burden *and* you have interest payments on the debt. It becomes harder and harder to get ahead. If you have cash reserves, you can weather a couple of bad months and make sure you are prepared to have good months in the future.

Staying Flexible

Your business is only truly stable when you are prepared for good times and bad. When times are good, no one wants to think about the market changes we all know are inevitable. During the real estate boom, everyone wanted to believe that housing prices would continue to rise forever. We all want our good month to be our "new normal," instead of looking realistically at the last 12 to plan for the next 12. We've all had closings delayed or derailed because of blizzards, hurricanes and other uncontrollable disasters. But when you save half of what you bring in, your team can weather a literal storm with no problem. Make it your goal to build your operating account to 6 months of cash reserves quickly by keeping a small budget and only spending on needs that bring in more revenue than they cost.

Just like with personal finances, paying down business debt trades off short term restrictions for long term freedom. Just like personal savings enable you to change jobs or careers easily, cash reserves do the same for your business. You can make quick adjustments in your company based on market conditions that you could never make otherwise.

Most of us like to think about our personal income and our business' income in the most favorable terms possible. We like to feel like we have a lot. So when we get a raise, we like to think about the things we can buy, rather than the taxes we'll owe. It's the same with a business: if we have a good month, we only think about the increased revenue, not the taxes and other costs of doing business. And ultimately, the same attitude that would cause someone to run up $10,000 on a personal credit card will cause a broker to over leverage his business and posture it for decline.

Leveraging Your Time and Money Well

Once you've got your spending under control and you are consistently bringing in more money than you need to cover your expenses, it's time to start putting your money to work. Leveraging your time and money will look different at every level of your growth as a real estate agent. At the beginning, it may simply mean paying someone a few bucks to pick up your yard signs and lockboxes so that you can spend those hours on more dollar productive activities. You may put money into marketing to generate more leads, adding to the calls you can make to generate appointments.

The simplest way to bring in more cash in real estate is to do more transactions and do them quickly. Once you're a team leader, you can start having buyers' agents work for you. There is no way you can be at ten open houses over the weekend, but you can have ten agents at ten open houses, leveraging the homes you've listed. They'll leverage those open houses to make deals with buyers, whom they'll then leverage to get referrals for more deals in the future.

In order to know how many agents to add, you'll need to watch your operating account balance. How well adding buyers' agents leverages your money depends on the model your brokerage uses.

At 1st Class Real Estate, we only charge team leaders $100 per agent, ensuring that bringing on new agents is a win-win proposition. Remember, you need to look for a model that utilizes fees (as opposed to commission splits) that demonstrate your broker is betting on your success, not trying to get all the money up front.

Your buyers' agents are more than just friendly faces: they each bring their own sphere of influence to your business. That's why it's rarely a good idea to hire a bunch of your friends to come work for you. If you all have the same set of acquaintances, you're not maximizing your reach. On the other hand, if you hire a former police officer, a former school teacher and someone retired from the military, you can leverage your new agents to gain entry into three completely different spheres of influence.

As you hire more agents, you will have to factor in increased expenses for running your business. In addition to the fees you pay on your agents, you'll need more office space and more staff to take care of all the time-consuming tasks associated with closing deals. This includes paperwork, data entry, marketing and other day-to-day details. While support staff cost money, they also free you and your agents up to deal directly with the clients that are bringing in the cash.

No one sells 500 homes a year alone. The simplest way to do it is to get about 20 agents each selling about 25 homes a year. That means you'll eventually need to hire more than 20 agents, since some of them inevitably drop out of the process. If you were counting on their ability to do transactions for you, you'll lose money if you don't have anyone ready to produce in their places.

Leverage doesn't stop with your buyers' agents. When you have enough volume, you can often begin to leverage it with other companies. For example, you can negotiate marketing agreements with mortgage companies: they may be happy to pay for some of your leads because you're sending them so much business. You can negotiate similar agreements with title companies, landscaping firms and any other business that benefits from what you do.

You will also want to keep tabs on how you are leveraging your time in your personal life. For example, if you know that you make about $100 an hour closing real estate deals it may not make sense to spend an hour mowing your lawn. Of course your lawn has to get cut, but you could probably hire someone to do it for $35. You could spend that extra hour working, or you could spend it attending your daughter's play. The goal is to spend your working hours doing the most dollar productive activities, while spending your personal time enjoying your family. That's how you keep your life balanced—even when things get really busy—and ensure you are making time for what matters most.

Chapter 9:

Systems

When I became a team leader, I knew I needed to get my phone to ring. After all, if the buyers aren't calling, no one is making money. But 12,000 minutes a month later, I wanted to throw my phone in the trash. Phone calls were monopolizing every moment of my day from the time I fed my daughter breakfast in the morning to the time I tried to help her with her homework at night. I needed a system, and I was going to have to come up with it myself.

Systems are essential to the health of your business. Just like we all function more effectively in our personal lives when we follow established routines, our businesses will run much more efficiently when we have established systems for everything that needs to be done. Good systems are also the key to living the balanced life that we all want, because the more efficient you are at work, the more time you can have with your family.

But systems can also take on lives of their own. Consider this: why aren't the real estate teams doing the largest volume of business always the most profitable? In addition to overspending on luxury items for the office, some may have 15 support staff for 30 agents, so the business they generate is getting swallowed up by salaries. In other cases, the owner may have spent tens of thousands of dollars on a customized software program to handle their leads, only to find it obsolete in a few years. Don't think spending more money will automatically get you a better system. Look carefully at the needs of your business and find the most cost effective way to build systems that will meet them.

No system is more important than the overall goals it is supposed to support. The database for your clientele should never be a higher priority than actually making contact with the people whose names it contains. The system for preparing paperwork for closing will never be more critical than ensuring that you have a steady stream of deals that actually close.

So you really don't want to go into debt to commission a software package you can't afford or hire six office support staff if three will give you enough room for growth. Furthermore, the real estate market is dynamic enough that you will need to tweak or adjust your systems on a regular basis. If the system is too rigid, you won't be able to do this easily. Remember, the system is the servant, not the master.

Getting Started

Why do people buy McDonald's franchises? Do they really think the company makes the world's best hamburgers and fries? Chances are good that your neighbor can make a better hamburger than McDonald's. People buy franchises because they offer proven models for profitability. It's not the secret recipe or the eleven herbs and spices: it's the systems. While I don't expect you to build systems at the level that McDonald's does, you can build sys-

146

tems that will enable you to be stable and flexible as your business grows.

For example, we developed a highly efficient, low cost system to coordinate our team duty schedule. This isn't so hard in an office with a handful of agents and a dozen properties, but we have more than 20 agents and 80-100 active listings at any given time. The challenge is to be available to our clients 24/7 without forcing everyone to work around the clock.

Developing better systems will make you more efficient, more productive and ultimately more competitive. It can also help the culture of your office, aid in recruiting quality agents and you can even use it to educate clients about the process of home buying and selling and why you are able to offer them better results. We set up our team duty schedule similar to a doctor's on-call schedule with a hospital. We have three shifts: 9:00 AM to 1:00 PM, 1:00 PM to 5:00 PM and 5:00 PM to the next morning, Monday through Saturday. During a shift, the agent on duty handles all the calls and emails that come in from buyers or buyers' agents. Every agent takes about 5-7 shifts a month, and only one of those will be a night on the weekend.

We have a central database with all the details of every property, including showing instructions and the agent in charge. This way, when a new buyer calls, the agent on duty has all the information he or she needs to serve the customer. Our customers are served immediately, our buyers' agents get more clients, and they get to spend the majority of their time showing properties on their own schedule and/or spending time with their families.

Calibrate Expectations

Many agents struggle to make the jump to team leader or broker because they feel like they don't have perfect systems in place. This is a little like saying you're not ready to have a child because you don't know everything about parenting. None of us know everything about parenting before we have children. But hopefully we know enough, and we learn the rest as we go along.

Instead of waiting until you develop the perfect system for everything (which you'll eventually have to change anyway), be honest with your team members that you're learning as you go. When you need to hire new people, it's very tempting to promise them the moon. But this is just setting them up to be disappointed in you. It's much better to under-promise and over-deliver.

When I started hiring agents, I tried to be very clear that they were going to have to be patient and grow with me as I developed the systems we were going to use. I let them know that I didn't have it all together but that my highest priority was their success. This set their expectations at a level I could not just meet but exceed.

I also learned early on—thanks to great advice from my wife—that you want all your systems, including your company traditions, to be set up for growth. For example, when I first went out on my own, I wanted to take the team out for dinner and drinks on Fridays. I really wanted a tangible way to show my appreciation for what they were doing, and I wanted that to be part of our company culture.

However, my wife pointed out that once I had twenty or thirty agents, it would no longer be feasible to take everyone out each week. She explained that if I set the expectation early on that this was how I showed my appreciation, they would feel let down if the tradition no longer continued.

Balance Efficiency with Profitability

As we discussed in the last chapter, you want to free yourself and your agents to do the most dollar-productive activities: meeting with clients and closing deals. But at the same time, you cannot start spending money on systems that your budget account won't allow. Even after selling 900 homes in a year, I still try to run my company as "skinny" as possible.

This is why I always advise team leaders to hire agents before they hire administrative support staff. This might seem counterintuitive. You should get all your systems in place and then expand, right? Well, if you hire staff before you have the revenue to sustain them, your company may not survive a year. If you have to choose between being overwhelmed with business and being overwhelmed with business debt, you're much better off with too much business.

Keep Technology in Perspective

Many amazing software packages can greatly increase your company's efficiency when it comes to marketing, keeping track of leads, and getting all the details together for each new deal. But before you break the bank buying the most expensive one out there (or paying to have a system custom-built for you), keep a few important facts in mind. First, most software packages will become obsolete as the market or the needs of your company change, and it is impossible to know what those changes will be. Typically, if you're thrilled with the software you're using today, you can expect to use it for about three years. Second, people bought and sold houses long before anyone developed electronic spreadsheets or

Google alerts. Remember, the software can make your job easier, but it doesn't personally connect with a client or close a deal. Those are the activities that generate cash for your business, and no computer program—no matter how sophisticated or expensive—will ever replace the human touch. Your business can survive without the software, but it can't survive if you're not closing enough deals.

Analyze Your Needs

When setting up your systems and deciding how much to spend, it's important to take a holistic look at your company's needs. The administrative tasks involved in real estate fall into six basic categories:

1. Marketing

In the old days, marketing primarily involved flyers and newspaper ads for the homes you were selling, along with (possibly) some billboards and bus, television or radio ads for general company recognition. All these forms of promotion are still in use today, but internet advertising has overtaken them all. In fact, 90% of real estate clients are found online. Paper ads remain in use mostly to please sellers, but they rarely produce any traffic to the property. For the most part, "old fashioned" marketing techniques like these are used strictly for very high-end listings.

Billboards and other media ads are largely for branding, as they offer so few ways to capture any leads or to determine your actual return on investment. They may be useful for some agents, but they are so expensive that I would not use them until you are well-established and have detailed guidance from someone who has used them successfully. I suggest reading *Purple Cow* or *Guerrilla Marketing* to get more tips and advice.

Today of course, every company has to have a presence on the internet and on social media as well. These forms of advertising allow you to run a cost-effective, focused marketing campaign rather than an expensive general campaign. Sites like Facebook,

Twitter and Instagram now allow you to reach specific demographics very easily. Don't skip this!

They also allow your company to appear larger and more dominant than it actually is. By boosting your Facebook posts, for example, you reach your potential customers several times, giving them the impression that you are "everywhere." If you are not using social media, you are giving up a large amount of referral business and low cost branding to your competition.

The more omnipresent your company appears, the more customers you attract. This allows you to *Explode* much faster and for less money. In addition to Facebook and Twitter, one of the most important forms of web presence today is pay-per-click advertising, like Google AdWords. This is local advertising that brings your ad to the top of the page whenever customers in your local area perform an internet search for keywords that involve buying or selling a house. Here are a few resources that I recommend:

https://support.google.com/adwords/?hl=en#to pic=3119071

https://support.google.com/adwords/answer/17 04341?hl=en

You have many options when it comes to your internet presence. You can build your own site, or you can pay a monthly fee for site like Tiger Leads or Boomtown that coordinates the pay-per-click with your leads database. There are advantages and disadvantages to both approaches.

A real estate website needs three major features: an IDX (internet data exchange) feed, SEO (search engine optimization) and a user interface. The IDX feed allows MLS properties to appear on your site. SEO (like pay-per-click) allows local buyers to find your company during internet searches and the user interface allows you to capture their contact information (discussed more in the next section). If you build your own site, you will need to purchase a domain name (through GoDaddy or a similar company), an IDX feed (through Zillow,

155

Trulia, iHomefinder or a similar company) and your pay-per-click advertising (though Google Adwords or a similar company).

As of today, website hosting starts at $10 a month, an IDX feed can cost about $60 a month and a lead management system can cost around $30 for an individual or $100 for a team. You can set your own budget for pay-per-click. You can also pay extra to become a premier agent on websites like Zillow or Trulia, which enables your listings to get more views, which can convert to leads. Companies like Tiger Leads or Boomtown will set up a site for you, but they typically charge a fee that far exceeds what it costs to buy the services individually.

Marketing in real estate today is less about getting your company's name out there and more about getting as many leads as you can in your market and managing them well. Think of it like throwing a net into the water to catch a school of fish swimming by. Most people agree that you should be able to convert 10% of your leads into sales. Use this to guide your budget: you will need 100 leads over the course of a year to close 10 deals, and you'll need 1000 to close 100. Obviously the higher your conversion rate is, the better. Unfortunately, internet leads tend to close at a lower rate than phone calls.

The dominance of the internet in real estate highlights how vital training is. Buyers are able to get almost any information they want online without the help of an agent. Your agents need to be undeniable experts on every aspect of the transaction to bring value to educated buyers. This is where training pays dividends. A well trained agent converting 1-2% more over a year can offer a much larger return.

2. Lead Cultivation And Follow Up

Obtaining and keeping track of the names and contact information of past, current and potential clients includes a huge number of tasks, from answering phone calls and emails to setting up and coordinating appointments. Before computers, people stored names and numbers in notebooks or rolodexes. Today, there are multiple computer systems that

157

can store information about your clients, costing anywhere from a couple hundred to tens of thousands of dollars.

While you will definitely want a quality database, remember that the database itself does not generate deals. Deals are generated by the personal connection between the agent and the client, so that has to remain your top priority. And regardless of which system you purchase, you will need a live human being to facilitate the follow up.

It is also vital that your system enables you to monitor your leads during the cultivation period. This will enable you to uncover any weak spots in your processes or in particular agents. The best way to do this is to break down the process—from first contact to conversion—and define the goal for each step. For example, the goal of an internet lead is to get a phone number. The goal of a phone number is to get an appointment. The goal of the appointment is to sign the person as your client (either as a buyer or a seller). If you sign a seller, then the lead is converted. Now you need to sell the property (which is another process you need to monitor). If you sign a buyer, you will still need to find the client a home, write a contract and then close.

You want to develop a system that allows you to handle and monitor this process effectively. As of now, Top Producer is cost effective, but it requires a little more work to use. InfusionSoft, Sales Force or Follow Up Boss are other options. Research them carefully to determine which one will meet your needs.

Remember, each deal is worth thousands of dollars. Your software can never make up for weak human follow-up, but it should show you where your weaknesses are so you can correct them. As with anything else, decide how much you are able to spend and work with what you can afford.

3. Paperwork Associated with Closing

In addition to the contract of a sale itself, there are a number of documents that need to be prepared, submitted and filed in order for a house to close. It's a good idea to go paperless as quickly as possible, since those document costs add up. This includes the title, the termite certificate (where applicable), the appraisal and associated document of home inspection and walk through, repair invoices, survey and other communications. You will need a reliable person to ensure that all these papers are in order so that there are no surprises at closing. Electronic spreadsheets do the math for you, greatly reducing computing errors, which can cost you thousands. In the unlikely event that someone enters the data incorrectly, the spreadsheet should make the error easier to catch.

Dotloop (*https://www.dotloop.com/*) has some great features which allow you to share loops as well as archive information. However, we have found a system called Skyslope (*https://app.skyslope.com/*) is better for our needs. It allows you to create a checklist for all contracts and listings and requires an approval for the file to move forward. This way one person can manage all the files for a lot of agents at one time. It has also released a lot of other features, such as DocuSign and Excel spreadsheets, which automate processes we were previously doing manually. Using Skyslope ultimately increased our capacity and lowered our overhead.

4. Bookkeeping

Stay close to the numbers! That's what my mentor would always say to me. Because of the countless tax and legal liabilities associated with real estate deals, you absolutely cannot neglect bookkeeping. You must ensure that you have accurate records of every transaction and every dollar that comes through your company. Furthermore, your bookkeeper shouldn't be the only one to see these numbers. I make sure to take time each day to see what is going on in every single account to confirm that the balances are what they should be.

Each day, I receive an email with the available balance in each of my accounts, as well as any checks written that day. This allows me to monitor closely for mistakes or problems. We use Payday Payroll to handle our payroll, but any reputable company is fine. Reports should be sent monthly or quarterly to your CPA to ensure your 1099's are processed on time, your taxes are paid and any errors are caught early.

Having an in-house bookkeeper you trust is absolutely vital. If you're just starting out and haven't been able to hire anyone yet, apps like Foreceipt can be helpful for tracking business expenses. Ultimately, keeping track of your finances daily will alleviate a lot of stress.

5. Recruiting

"Recruiting solves all your problems!"

That was the best advice a competing broker ever gave me. It was not until years later I realized how true it was. Recruiting allows you to adjust when you have set something in place that you no longer want - like a commission structure. The new agent doesn't know about the old way that wasn't working. It also breeds healthy competition within your company, as the older agents automatically feel motivated to do a good job so they will get handed leads.

Your system for recruiting and hiring should make it easy to bring in new employees. I personally enjoy hiring, so I use my own account in Follow Up Boss to manage my agent recruits. Begin each recruiting relationship with a 30 minute appointment to explain the value you offer. Just like with leads, you want to monitor each stage of the process from first contact to hire.

Recruiting, while sometimes overwhelming, is one of your most vital activities. It forces you to train and forces you to bring in more business, so make it a priority. Broker Metrics is a software package that allows you to pull the MLS stats of any agent you want to hire, as well as their contact information. Examining their sales numbers will help you see which seasoned agents meet your standards. You can also get the local real estate schools to send you a list of new agents each month. Remember, some of these are quality people who could thrive in your company. Don't let them slip away. In addition to a good recruiting system, you'll need a standard-ized way to onboard new agents. We send a standard email each time a new agent comes onboard that looks like this:

All,

Jeff Duncan is a new agent joining the team!! He is excited to get started with his training while he awaits his license!!

Jeff, your company email to log in through gmail.com is Jeff@1stClassAgents.com. Temporary PW is #$%^. Please change that when you log in :) I've added you to the team email so your inbox will fill up fast. Some of them won't make sense yet, but be sure to open them all so you don't miss anything important.

Please see me for an office key when you come in. The office alarm code is ++++. Please text/call me if you have any access issues after hours. 757-717-XXXX

Jane Doe is the Finch team Sales Manager and will be your "go to" person.

Emily S. is our transaction coordinator and will take great care of all of your closings.

Chrissy G. is our listing coordinator and will ensure all listing documents are on file.

Shane B. is our full time courier and will assist you with listing pictures, signs and lockboxes.

Alexis G. is our front desk receptionist and will assist you with getting set up on the wifi and printers.

Susan S. is up front as well; she handles our property management division.

Jane will get you all set up with training and information you need to know.

Chrissy, please order his business cards once he sends you a picture.

Alexis please add Jeff to the company roster and calendars.

Email: Jeff@1stClassAgents.com

Mobile # is 757-477-XXXX

Efax: 757-431-XXXX

Mailbox Ext for office: XYZ

We look forward to working with you!!!

6. Training

You need a system for your training too. Have a set of items agents must know before they start. We call ours the 1st Class Ticket. Our team agents get training on our systems and how we handle calls and leads. This may seem very basic, but it is valuable to new agents coming in. We also do company training once a month on topics like new technology; for example, not long ago, we taught our team to use smart phones and tablets for contract writing.

Stay Flexible

You want to build systems that offer both stability and flexibility. If you change the way you do everything all the time, you'll be extremely inefficient, wasting time and money. But if you are rigid and unable to adjust, you'll become obsolete. The key is to find the right balance.

The real estate market is constantly shifting. What worked this year may not work next year. Whenever you have a new idea, you'll need to be able to adjust your systems to accommodate it. When we began selling REO properties, we had to develop a whole new way to keep track of renovations and other benchmarks we had to hit for our clients. You'll have similar challenges as you go along.

Good systems allow you to live the life you want and avoid the chaotic schedule of the typical real estate agent. With the right systems you can keep your processes efficient, poise your business for growth, and have time for the people you value most.

Chapter 10:

Expansion

Expansion isn't for everyone.

Most people who establish a team with 20 to 30 agents selling 500 houses a year have succeeded beyond their wildest dreams. And truthfully, this is the point at which most people are content. Once you have your systems in place and running smoothly, you should be working exactly as much as you want to. You should be doing the parts of your business you enjoy the most and spending quality time with your family.

But a small percentage of people who achieve this level of success will still be restless, because they know they have not yet fulfilled their potential. Their hunger to grow their business further goes beyond merely wanting more income; they know they have more to offer the industry and the world. They possess a combination of drive, vision and a desire to have an impact beyond just the confines of one local office.

If this describes you, you will want to run multiple offices or franchise your business. This chapter will cover the factors you need to consider if expansion is in your future.

Risk Assessment

Expansion involves risk, so you need to make sure that your current office is running smoothly first. That means you have a consistent revenue stream over a 12-month cycle and you are no longer involved in the day-to-day procedural details. You have successfully hired and trained people to do all the vital tasks involved in running your office, and you should no longer be hiring, training or dealing directly with clients unless there is an emergency or a special situation.

To expand you also need to have enough cash in reserves to weather a storm—an economic downturn or a shift in the market. As I've said several times, I think you should have a 6-month reserve minimum. But more than that, you should be looking at which parts of your business are producing residual income. Have you established an REO account? Do you have a new construction site? Have you served investors who are now buying and selling or buying and holding with you? Do you have a property management division? Endeavors like these allow for consistent income as you expand.

It is also my personal opinion that before you expand, your first team should be in a building that you own. Owning your building protects you from throwing money away on rent or on renovations and improvements on a rental property. It also allows you to write off the interest on the mortgage, while the value of your property should continue to rise.

Ultimately, whether or not you take the risk involved in expansion is a personal gut check: are you ready and willing? Is this step gambling or a sensible investment? Is it worth the extra stress and pressure?

All these are questions you have to answer for yourself.

Trademark

If you think you want to continue expanding in the future, it's a good idea to trademark your company name. This involves a small fee and simple paperwork and prevents any branding confusion as you head into less familiar locales. You can do this on your own or have an attorney do it for roughly $750. Below is the firm I used for this:

Law Offices of Carl Khalil & Sada Sheldon
2000 General Booth Blvd, Suite 201
Virginia Beach, VA 23454
757-263-4596
www.khalilsheldon.com

Location

So where should you open up your next office? It is probably not a good idea to set up shop right down the street, since you don't want your two offices duplicating efforts or competing for the same clientele. At the same time, the farther away your second office is, the more logistical challenges you will face. Finding the balance can be tricky.

Most people agree that your second office should be at least 30 miles away. There can be special reasons to go a little farther: maybe you have contacts or relationships in a city that's 60 miles away, for example. But unless you plan to move your personal residence, you will want to stay within comfortable driving distance if at all possible.

Once you decide on a location, you are going to repeat the process you went through setting up your first office. Of course since you have experience (and plenty of cash in reserve), the process won't necessarily take as long as it did the first time. But just like your first office, you'll let your budget account dictate how quickly you progress.

We now have amazing technology that makes managing a business remotely much easier than it used to be. You can use video conferencing and other webcam technology to stay in touch with your people and properties, even when you're not physically there. Still, distance will bring its share of challenges. Not all the businesses you have relationships with—from title companies to inspectors and contractors—will be able to drive to your new location, and those that are will face added commute time.

Lease or Buy?

One of the first decisions you'll need to make when you open a new office is whether you want to buy or lease office space. Some brokers who are expanding decide to lease for a year or two and see how quickly they grow before they purchase. Others may lease or purchase more space than they immediately need and try to fill it quickly. When I started my second office, I rented a small place off the beaten path. This allowed me to save money for my purchase. These choices really come down to how quickly you realistically think you'll grow and how much you are comfortable risking.

Hiring

Obviously you will need to hire buyers' agents just like you did in your first office. Then you are back to the listing/hiring/training cycle until you are ready to train and promote agents to do it for you. At this point you won't have your hand in every deal that your new team does, so you will have to be comfortable giving up a measure of control. You will also need to factor in any errors that your new team members make as they adjust to your system.

One of the challenges you will most likely face in your new office is that you don't have the same established level of influence that you've built up with your original team. That's okay, but they will need inspiration and leadership from somewhere. Ideally, you should train someone from within your company to fulfill this role.

Multiple Offices or Franchise?

Opening additional offices is an exciting but highly individual experience. There's no way to predict exactly how it's going to go, so you have to set realistic goals, watch your budget account and honestly assess your progress. By saving 50 percent of everything that comes in and taking your risks with cash, you ensure that the venture won't bankrupt you, but you may also decide you need to pull back if the new office is more trouble than it's worth. That's not a problem: you can always try again somewhere else.

Once your new office is up and running successfully, you have a choice. You can stop there, you can continue to open new offices yourself or you can become a franchise. If you decide to keep opening and running your own offices, you can continue to expand 30 miles down the road, or you can go to cities where you may have contacts or influence.

If you decide to become a franchise, you will package your systems and training and sell it to other brokers for franchise fees and royalties. This means that you will need to hire and pay people to travel and train new brokers and agents, or you can do it yourself. The choice will come down to how quickly your franchise grows and how much time you want to spend on the road.

Either way, expansion will lead to opening offices in other states. As I mentioned earlier, laws governing real estate transactions vary from state to state, so opening a branch in a new state will require something called "foreign qualification." Consult your attorney and your accountant to prepare these documents.

What's Next?

Once you've expanded to multiple offices in multiple states or become a successful franchise, the "last frontier" is to become a publicly traded company. Obviously, this allows you to hold an IPO to sell shares while retaining a majority stake in the company. It also allows you to sell your shares when you are ready to retire.

Again, most people in real estate are very happy leading a team of 20 to 30 agents selling 500 homes a year. They stay profitable, they find their work rewarding and they are able to keep their stress level to a minimum. Expansion is not necessary; it's just an option for people who want more - those who truly want to *EXPLODE*. If you decide to expand, make sure you are doing it for the right reasons and at a pace that allows you to keep your priorities intact.

Thank You

Thank you for reading this book. I truly hope it was beneficial and that it enables you to find professional success without sacrificing your personal life. I would like to close with a few personal thoughts about the most important part of my life.

I came from a family of limited means and made some very poor choices early in life. In addition to being a plumber, I sold drugs and hung out with the wrong people. When I had my daughter, I didn't only want to give her a better life: I wanted to be a better man.

God saved me and redeemed me. I didn't deserve it, but I gave my heart to Him, and by His grace He set me on a course to help change people's lives. I didn't write this book to make money but to give people hope. This true story is just a small part of all God has taught me and continues to teach me every day. I know I'm not special, and I truly believe that anyone can find the success I've had.

You may be new to real estate, trying to decide if this is the right path for you, or maybe you've been in it for a while but are struggling to make ends meet. My hope is you can do an even better job than I have done. But all of this is meaningless if we succeed professionally but have no positive impact on others. Our company works to give back to the community by offering financial peace seminars to the public, giving to various charities, feeding the less fortunate on holidays and even paying delinquent mortgages in special circumstances. So I leave you with the motto of my company: *We are changing lives and selling a few homes along the way.*

If you want to share in our vision we would love to hear from you. Feel free to reach out to us at:

Join@1stclassre.com

www.1stclassre.com

Additional Resources:

My buddy Josh Smith has incredible education to help you crush it in your real estate business. Find out more at www.JoshuaSmithGSD.com

Recommended Reading:

Serve To Be Great (Matt Tenny)

The Go Giver (Bob Burg and John David Mann)

The 7 Levels of Communication (Michael Maher)

Rich Dad Poor Dad (Robert Kiyosaki)

The Richest Man in Babylon (George S. Clason)

The Total Money Makeover (Dave Ramsey)

The Purpose Driven Life (Rick Warren)

The E-myth (Michael E. Gerber)

Take the Stairs (Rory Vaden)

Guerilla Marketing (Jay Conrad Levinson)

Live Rich by Spending Smart (Gregory Karp)

How Real Estate Debt Can Make You Rich

(Steve Dexter)

Cash Flow Quadrant (Robert Kiyosaki)

Appendix A:

More Tips for Handling REO Accounts

Get In

Getting an account like Fannie Mae starts with relationship building. You have to be able to persistently pursue the right people and be resilient in the face of rejection. The gatekeepers at Fannie Mae are the sales representatives in your market. And trust me, when you figure out who that individual is and try to connect, you will not be the only one vying for attention.

You need to get to know your potential REO account better than you ever got to know any family whose home you were selling. Contrary to what you might think, the relationship building doesn't stop after you become an approved REO agent. There are REO agents right now that hardly ever get handed properties. Why? Because the people in charge want to give properties to the agents that they believe can enable them to meet their threshold for that month. You must cultivate and take care of that relationship to make sure that you are one of those agents.

Here is how the application process for Fannie Mae or Freddie Mac goes for most people:

You fill out an application, and if you don't know exactly what they're looking for, that will be the end of it. Remember, nothing Fannie Mae asks you is for the purpose of getting to know you better. They are looking for specific answers, and if you don't know those answers, game over.

If you fill the application out correctly, it can still sit around on someone's desk for months. Then, with no warning, you get a call for a phone interview, a call from a stranger who asks you a bunch of counterintuitive questions. You do your best to answer, but you have no sense of whether the interview is going well or poorly. Then you hear nothing for weeks or even months. Finally, you learn if you've been accepted or rejected, often with no explanation.

Two things made the difference for me. First, I knew how to fill out the application. Second, when I got the call for the interview six months later, I got the contact information for the person that interviewed me. That enabled me to follow up over the next several months, during which my original interviewer switched territories, so I had to hassle two different people. But finally I was given a shot.

This is the best way to navigate the process:

1. Fill out the application correctly. Looking back on it, I was very, very fortunate to ever get a call.

2. Go to the decision maker. This saves the six months I had to wait to get the initial interview.

3. Go through the phone interview. I coach all my agents on what questions to expect and how to answer them correctly.

4. Wait while the interviewer submits your application.

5. Wait while a manager approves your application.

6. Wait while a vendor manager approves your application.

Once you've navigated these steps, you're in the door and the "real" application process begins. You will fill out the paperwork again, but this time they'll be going behind you checking up on all the details. Your business must meet certain requirements and demonstrate adequate insurance coverage and so on. If you have anything in your background (or if your broker has anything on his or her license) that can be a problem. But if everything checks out okay, they will start sending you listings.

What does it Take?

So now you've invested all the time and effort to cultivate the right relationships with the right people. But the fact remains that without performance, relationships mean nothing.

Remember, it takes a different set of skills and priorities to be a successful REO agent than it does to be a traditional re-sale agent. This is intensified with a client like Fannie Mae because they are not going to bend their standards for anyone. I can't emphasize it enough: you could be the number one agent in your market, but if you don't play by Fannie Mae's rules (and remember, those rules are unreasonable!), they will suspend you without thinking about it twice.

I've watched agents who were very, very successful in traditional re-sales lose their Fannie Mae accounts. In fact, I was brought on at a time when very good agents were being terminated nationwide for performance reasons. Why? More often than not because they tried to do business the way they were used to doing it, instead of understanding the way Fannie Mae was evaluating them. They thought they were doing everything right, but they were digging their own graves.

It's sort of like going to the professor to find out what's on the test before you start studying. If you don't do that, you can waste a lot of time on things that don't matter very much. To know how to exceed Fannie Mae's expectations, you need to be constantly aware of the specific criteria they are using to evaluate you. Then you can tailor your priorities to ensure you will get a good evaluation.

After the nationwide termination that opened the door for me, Fannie Mae updated the score card it used for all its agents. Not surprisingly, it reflects the criteria it used to evaluate its sales representatives. It contains four criteria: EMV, Sales Runoff, Disposition and Sales Conversion. When Fannie Mae distributes their assets, they are looking for agents who can get high marks in these four areas. If you don't do them well one month, you will get a poor scorecard. If you get two poor scorecards in a row, you'll be suspended indefinitely, which is basically the same as being fired.

Understanding the Difference

Traditional re-sales involve a particular set of incentives for the buyer and seller and a corresponding set of skills for the agent. Some of these are concepts we learned about in the real estate class, and others are intuitions we develop as we go. We all know that the typical family selling a home will be emotionally attached to it. Their children grew up there; they've enjoyed countless holidays in front of that fireplace. A low offer isn't merely a financial issue; it feels like a personal insult, devaluing their memories.

From a financial standpoint, traditional home sellers want to make as much money as possible on their home, since it is typically one of their largest assets. Depending on their circumstances, they may be content to wait for a while rather than accept an offer that is too low. While waiting, their house is still meeting their basic need for shelter. So as long as they're maintaining it properly, they're not "losing" any money.

An effective agent is acutely aware of these emotional and financial subtexts and helps to get sellers and buyers over the various obstacles. Ideally, they reach a point of agreement that is a win for everyone involved. These are skills we hone for months, or even years, in traditional re-sales, and they are almost totally useless for an REO transaction.

With REO properties, the family is long gone and the bank is the seller. The agent is using his or her skills to mitigate loss for the bank. The bank is not emotionally attached to the property any more than Toyota is emotionally attached to a particular Camry. Each home is probably one of thousands of assets they are dealing with. A low offer is evaluated purely from a financial standpoint, and the longer the house sits there, the more money the bank loses.

There are differences on the seller side too. Traditional buyers may be at almost any stage of life: first time home buyers, middle aged folks upgrading or retirees looking for a single level home to host their grandchildren. Like everyone, they want to get the most for their money, but many may be interested in factors like school districts and gated communities. Good agents will help buyers find homes that not only provide the right number of bedrooms and bathrooms but also offer the right neighborhood and other amenities.

REO buyers are very often first time homebuyers, and all of them expect to get a lot for their money. Furthermore, REO properties carry a particular stigma—the image of the rundown foreclosure that the bank is desperate to unload. A good REO agent needs to help buyers overcome that stigma and see that foreclosure does not necessarily reflect poorly on the home's potential. They help calibrate a buyer's understanding of a "good deal" against market realities, while directing them to the best home that meets their needs.

Successful REO agents understand all these differences and are able to adjust their tactics and approach accordingly. They are able to let go of their old ways of thinking and approach REO transactions with the bank's goals in mind. You could be the best re-sale agent in your market, but if you don't modify your frame of reference, you will struggle in the REO market.

Understanding Your Client

There are three nightmare agents for the bank. The first is the guy who just wants to list everything too low, leave everything un-repaired and move the properties quickly. While this strategy gets the properties off the books, it can cause the bank to take unnecessary losses. The second is the agent who tries to get the higher price and lets the properties sit around for months. Those homes may end up selling for higher prices, but the bank takes losses by maintaining them for so long. The third is the agent that may manage the sales process reasonably well but can't keep up with all the repairs and maintenance to get newer properties ready to list.

The dream REO agent knows how to balance all of these competing factors on multiple properties in a way that allows the bank to lose the least amount of money that month. With that in mind, Fannie and Freddie do have demographic requirements (based on ethnicity and gender) for how they distribute their properties. Regardless, the best way (under your control) to get handed more properties is to perform well.

Preparing for Pre-sale

First things first: if you are in any way confused about the REO sale process, DO NOT call the bank and start asking questions. This will create the impression that you don't know what you're doing and cannot be trusted. If you are not completely sure what to do, you must have someone you can trust to provide the right answers.

For Fannie Mae properties, you must physically visit the property within a day of receiving it and create an Occupancy Status Report (OSR). Before driving out there, you MUST double-check the address in the tax records. Fannie Mae manages hundreds of thousands of REO properties, and sometimes they will give you an incomplete address or even the wrong address. This happens most often in densely populated urban areas, but it can happen anywhere. You do NOT want to go to the incorrect home and inform the occupants the bank has taken possession of their home, and you certainly don't want to drill out the wrong locks! If you have any doubt whatsoever about the address after double-checking, contact the foreclosure attorney for clarification.

If the property is vacant, then it is time to rekey the locks, check the utilities and work on creating a BPO. If the utilities are not on, double-check the breakers and main water valve and contact the appropriate person to get the utilities turned on. You will have to return to confirm that this is done; this is a top priority, so if the utilities aren't on by your second visit, you'll need to find out why. For example, is there damage to the pipes or an issue with the electrical system? The BPO clock has been ticking ever since you reported the property vacant, so you have no time to delay. The only reason to leave the utilities off is a safety concern, and this requires written permission from the bank.

If the home is occupied, you must have a talk with the occupants or leave a "Know Your Options" (KYO) brochure (in English and Spanish). There are three main options for former owners who still occupy a Fannie Mae foreclosure: they can receive a cash incentive to move right away (Cash for Keys/CFK), or they can purchase the property back from Fannie Mae. You must understand these options very well and explain them clearly, or the former owners can complain to their congressman and get you in a lot of trouble.

No one's house becomes an REO property because of a happy story. When you approach that home to meet with the former owners, you are most likely not going to be welcomed with open arms. Remember that you are there representing their former lender, and your visit is almost certainly the first physical contact they have had with their bank. Sure, the bank has been calling and sending them letters for months, but they probably haven't been answering the phone or opening the mail. For most occupants in this situation, this is a very stressful time.

Fannie Mae regulations (and good manners) require that you do everything possible to respect the dignity of the former owners. You are not concerned with how they came to lose their home. You are there to help them understand how to move on. Many of former owners are angry or scared; they may even think you are coming to throw all their furniture on the lawn like an eviction from a rental property. You are there to reassure them that they have options and to help them choose the right one.

Once they decide, you must update your sales representative and complete all the necessary paperwork (which you can download from Fannie Mae's website). You do not want to pressure the occupants into anything, but ultimately, you do want them out as soon as possible. Remember, you are mitigating loss for the bank, and the sooner they are out, the sooner the property can be sold.

Inspecting and Creating the BPO

Once the property is vacant, you need inspect it and confirm that all the trash and personal property has been removed. Unless you have special authorization from the bank in writing (usually due to mitigating circumstances such as a serious illness or unavoidable tragedy), there are no exceptions to this rule. In Fannie Mae properties, if there are any environmental hazards—asbestos, mold, biohazards and so on—you must follow Fannie Mae's very detailed procedures for securing entrance to the property and ordering any emergency repair.

Assuming there are no major issues with your inspection, you should submit your BPO within four days of entering the property into the system. The BPO is a three-page report in which you make your case to the bank for how the property should be priced and marketed. This is the hill you are dying on: if you go too high, the property will sit around too long. If you go too low, the bank loses too much on the sale. To do a BPO properly, you need to have a very detailed and nuanced understanding of the property itself, the neighborhood, the financing options and the market.

You must also be able to look at a property and know who the likely buyer for that property is. This will guide every decision you make for that property, whether it relates to market strategy or which specific types of renovations to make. If you know a house is going to be sold to an owner-occupant, then you know you'll need to make sure the roof and HVAC are in good shape. If you're selling to an investor, you're typically going to sell "as-is" for cash.

Once you've moved a few hundred properties, you can almost always predict the buyer as soon as you see the property. Will it be an investor, a first time home buyer, a middle aged married couple or retirees? Will they pay cash or use financing? If financing, what kind? These demographic details guide the creation of your BPO. We will look at the BPO creation process in complete detail in the next chapter.

Maintenance and Repair

Fannie Mae assigns a Field Services vendor to perform initial and ongoing maintenance services, as well as minor safety-related repairs. These might include fixing loose steps, repairing a minor plumbing leak, capping a wire and so on. Of course the companies and specific services vary from region to region, but most will cover trash removal, winterization, lawn maintenance and snow removal, as well as any emergency repairs. Agents are responsible for making sure the vendor completes all initial maintenance on a property. You must also inspect the property weekly to ensure its overall security and that the vendor is performing all the ongoing maintenance. After each visit, you need to update the files with the results of that inspection. If the property is still occupied, you can do a drive by inspection.

If your BPO involves repairs and renovations to the property, you must immediately complete a Broker Scope of Repair (BSOR) form. To do this properly, you must gather as much good information as possible about the condition of the property. This will include pictures taken during the walk through of the property, including wide shots of each room, as well as photos of details such as siding, trim, paint, carpet, appliances and so on.

Then you can begin to receive bids from contractors for the work, which should match the estimates on your BPO. Fannie Mae allows contractors three days to start and then one day per thousand dollars of repair to complete the job. Obviously this means you need to develop relationships with reliable professionals who can guarantee their work and complete it in a timely manner. If they can finish ahead of time with high quality work, that's even better. Keep in mind that Fannie Mae expects their agents to use Service Agreement Market (SAM) repair contractors for obtaining bids and performing the repairs if such contractors are available in your area.

No matter how large your repair budget, you must manage your contractors efficiently, tactfully and with authority. You must immediately address any issues that arise with communication, work quality and efficiency. Contractors *will* make mistakes; it's your job to catch those mistakes and resolve them right away. Fannie Mae has very high standards for the quality of repairs, so if you're not satisfied with the work, they won't be either. If the repair process drags on or comes in over budget, you can be sure your scorecard will be very negatively affected.

Once the repairs are complete, you must physically inspect the property and update all your files with new photos. This helps the bank know that the work is complete and reassures them that they got their money's worth. Again, you do not want to wait for the bank to contact you for this information; you want to be ahead of the game at all times.

Of course you are not an architect or even a home inspector, and no one expects you to be. But you should possess a general knowledge of how homes are built. You must know the difference between granite, laminate, and Silestone, as well as which brands of replacement windows and doors work best. You certainly need to be able to determine when a job has been done correctly.

Listing and Receiving Offers

You should personally review all offers and submit them to the bank. Once an offer on a Fannie Mae property is accepted, you must submit the contract for execution by Fannie Mae within five days, and the buyers must complete their inspection within ten days. Of course you must also ensure the buyers' loan has been approved before the financial contingency expiration date passes. And if you will be unable to meet the original closing date set, you must prepare a closing extension at least five days prior to the original date.

DO NOT GET YOUR SALES REPRE-SENTATIVE FIRED! Sales representatives can be terminated for accepting an investor offer within the first fifteen days a property is on the market. This is known as the "First Look" period, and Fannie Mae takes this policy very seriously. Because their mission is to sell to owner-occupants, any offer accepted during the First Look period must be from someone who intends to live in the property. Your sales representatives are relying on you to keep them in compliance, so if an offer comes in from an investor during this time, you MUST make special note of it.

Closing

You want the closing process to move quickly and smoothly. This means you must have all the key people in place: the title company, attorneys and so on. Prior to closing you must rekey the locks and submit the bill to the title company. You should also provide closing updates to your sales representative at least twice a month until closing is complete and review the HUD-1.

I realize that sounds like a lot of information, and honestly many brokers I have talked to simply don't believe that it takes jumping through all those hoops to succeed with an account like Fannie Mae, but it does. They are dead serious about their (unreasonable!) rules, and if you try to take short cuts, they will suspend you.

Appendix B:

Creating the Perfect BPO

This appendix details how to do BPO's Fannie Mae's way. And if you can do a perfect BPO for Fannie Mae, you can do one for anyone.

The BPO is what sets you up for failure or success, so you've got to get it right. The Fannie Mae manager assigned to you may be living a thousand miles away. Your BPO must clearly communicate the status and marketability of your property, and it must make a persuasive case for how you believe they should proceed.

You may have other conversations with Fannie Mae about the property, but this is your only chance to make your case on the record. Once your BPO is accepted, you can't re-do it for 90 days. And chances are, if 90 days has passed, no one is happy.

BPO Overview

The BPO is an online three-page report with several fields to fill out, divided into several main sections. They include:

1. Basic Information

This includes important details about the property, such as the REO number and address.

2. General Marketing Conditions

This is a professional assessment of the marketing conditions in the neighborhood, including housing prices, employment and so on.

3. Subject Marketability

This is a detailed assessment of the status of the home itself, size, condition and types of financing available.

4. Competitive Closed Sales and Active Comps

This is a list of three comparable properties recently sold and three comparable properties on the market, as well as a detailed assessment of all the features of those homes.

5. Marketing Strategy

*Very simply, this explains whether you recommend selling the property **As-Is**, **As-Repaired** or **Partial/Lender Required Repairs.***

6. Market Value

This is the selling price you recommend for the property.

7. Comments

This is where you explain anything in your BPO that needs explaining.

Marketing Strategy

Your marketing strategy basically encompasses how much money you recommend that Fannie Mae spend on a property in order to sell as quickly as possible for the highest possible price. You base this not only on the buyer profile you have in mind when you look at the property but also on the specific details of the neighborhood. How old are the houses? Which houses are for sale and what condition are they in?

Although the ideal Fannie Mae buyer is always an owner occupant, there are some properties that will need to be sold "as is" to investors. There are several factors that might make this the best option for the bank. Maybe nothing has moved in that neighborhood for a year. Maybe the house needs a new electrical system and new pipes in addition to normal repairs, making the cost of renovations prohibitive. Other expensive problems that make the home unmarketable include severe roof damage, structural issues and a non-functioning kitchen.

Most of the time, you will opt for at least minimal repairs. You will need to consider the time the repairs will take and the effect that time will have on your valuation report. You also need to think about the weather (January in Chicago is not the best time to put on a new roof!) and what you anticipate the market doing at the time the property is ready to list.

Your goal is to prioritize repairs that will make it competitive in its neighborhood. If the comparable houses are five years old, you are probably looking at just paint and carpet. If those houses are twenty years old, and all the houses for sale have new roofs and HVAC units, you'd better prioritize those. If none of the houses in the neighborhood have been upgraded or kept particularly well, just a little exterior paint and landscaping can make your property look like the most desirable home on the street.

The option to do minor to significant repairs opens up new pools of buyers both by making the property attractive and by making it eligible for different types of financing. The key is to understand which repairs will offer the best return in the sale price. Sometimes it's obvious: a broken window or stained carpet will turn off most buyers, but they are easily fixed. Visible, noxious mold in the basement may make a house unsellable to anyone but an investor. Yet a certified repair that might cost $15,000 in some areas could yield an increase in sale price of over $100,000.

Pictures

There is no set rule on how many pictures you need to include in a BPO, but generally speaking, the more the better. A good guideline is to take three pictures per room, five pictures of the exterior, plus a picture of anything that is damaged. That includes a loose shingle, flaking paint or a missing light fixture. So for a three bedroom townhouse, you probably need to include 50-60 pictures. Use a camera with at least 8 megapixels with at least a 4X optical zoom. Your pictures should include, but are not limited to:

- Front photo of home

- Rear photo of home

- Street scene

- 3 photos of each interior room from different angles

- 4-5 photos of the kitchen, including appliances, counters and any other details

- 1-2 photos of each utility, breaker panel, gas meter, electric meter, HVAC unit, boiler, hot water heater, etc.

- Light fixtures

- Plumbing fixtures

Take multiple photos of anything that will need repairs, looks broken or just doesn't look right. This includes, but is not limited to, interior and exterior siding, rotted trim and broken concrete. These photographs will help you remember every detail of the house, since you will most likely be managing multiple properties. They also show your sales representative that you are being thorough and paying attention to important details.

Comparable Properties

BPO's require detailed descriptions of three comparable properties recently sold and three comparable properties listed. In a perfect world, these would be properties on the same street with identical floor plans that sold within the past two months. In the real world, you must find houses that are as similar as possible. Houses in the same neighborhood with the same number of bedrooms and bathrooms that recently sold are acceptable. At a minimum, you should find homes with the same number of levels. It can be incredibly hard to compare a three level townhouse against a two level model, so avoid this if at all possible. Other important factors are age, garage vs. no garage and architectural style.

Everyone knows the importance of location. You need to stay in the same zip code if at all possible. If you go outside a five block radius in an urban area, you'd better explain why. If you're dealing with a rural area you might need to go two miles away, but that might be the only home of comparable size that sold within the last six months. All that is fine, but you must explain it in the comments section.

You must choose your comparable houses very carefully because they will determine the acceptable range for the selling price. If we are using an "as-is" marketing strategy, we typically use two "as-is" comps and one repaired. If we are using an "as-repaired" strategy, we use two repaired properties and one "as-is." But of course it always depends on what you have available. You can make appropriate adjustments for almost any difference, but the more similar the properties, the quicker and more accurate your BPO is likely to be.

Adjustments

Of course your comparable properties do not duplicate the condition and marketability of your property perfectly, so now you have to explain how and why you are adjusting the price of your property. If you believe your property should be listed at $230,000 and one of your comps sold for $300,000, you must explain in detail why you believe your property is worth $70,000 less. Maybe the comparable property had new carpet, new paint, new appliances and a larger basement. The bank understands everything about the property in terms of dollars, so you must explain what each of these is worth in your market and then correlate it to repair dollars.

There is no standard formula for adjustments, but whatever you do, you must be consistent within a particular market. If you say new carpet and interior paint is worth $20,000 in a repaired sales price, you need to stick to it. The bank will notice right away if you are claiming an extra bedroom is worth $5,000 more in sales price in one BPO and worth $25,000 more in another. If for any reason your adjustments are going to be inconsistent, you MUST justify your choice in detail in the comments section.

Winning and Losing

When you are moving REO properties for Fannie Mae, you will have disagreements with other professionals around you. This is particularly true when an appraiser comes in to offer his assessment of the appropriate market price for your property. It is not uncommon for an appraiser to come in higher than an agent and for Fannie Mae to choose the higher sales price. So what do you do?

Most of us think we've won an argument if we are proven right. Imagine you say Baltimore is 41 miles from Washington, DC, and I say it's 100 miles away. We look it up, and you're right. You win, right? Well, that mindset has gotten a lot of agents suspended from Fannie Mae.

If an appraiser comes up with a number different than yours, you have to know how to play your cards to make sure you win the outcome, not the argument. Let's say you are given a property that you judge to be worth $180,000 repaired but is in need of $35,000 of work. An appraiser looks at the same property and decides it is worth $190,000 repaired and needs only $20,000 of work. So you want to list the home for $130,000, and he wants to list it for $170,000. The bank understandably wants to go with the higher price.

Then there is the problem of financing, a huge issue for most of your buyers. Because the home needs more than $32,000 of work, it doesn't qualify for Fannie Mae's HomePath financing, a loan program that allows buyers benefits, such as lower down payments and forgoing mortgage insurance. It also doesn't qualify for HomePath Renovation financing. The buyer won't be able to get FHA, VA or conventional financing because the home won't pass inspection.

So you're stuck, and there are a few ways you can approach this situation. You can hope to sell it for cash, which is probably a long shot in this situation. Or you can throw up your hands and wait for the market to prove you right. In this scenario, you will lower the price each month until it sells at $130,000, exactly like you said it would. You won, right? You might think this outcome would make the bank trust your judgment in the future, but what it will do is cause them to give you a nice fat "F" on your scorecard.

Why? Because the property probably sat there for three or four months as you lowered the price to prove the appraiser wrong. This hurt one of your most important criteria for performance. You won the argument but lost the outcome. Remember when I told you the rules are unreasonable?

There is an alternative: you can negotiate with Fannie Mae to do some repairs. Now you have to know that they will not approve the full $35,000 in renovations. Remember, they are trying to mitigate loss, not go further in the hole. But maybe you can put in $10,000, enough to make it more appealing to your target seller and bring it above the threshold to make it eligible for certain financing options.

Now maybe you lower the price once and move it in a month for $160,000. You've just improved your scorecard immensely: you've opened up a much larger pool of buyers, it didn't sit around too long and you got a better price. In this scenario, you look like you "lost" the disagreement about the $130,000 listing price, but you won on your scorecard.

There are other situations where Fannie Mae agents can unwittingly cause themselves to lose. Suppose an offer comes in too low on a property. An agent could "win" in the short term by persuading Fannie Mae to take the offer. He makes the money on the transaction in the short term, but his scorecard will be affected negatively because of the size of the loss. Depending on the situation, he could get fewer properties the following month, or even be suspended. To be successful with Fannie Mae, you have to know where your monthly scorecard is at any given time and how each of the hundreds of decisions you make each month will affect it.

Again, I've watched very good agents turn in all their BPO's on time, do their weekly property checks and fulfill their obligations to Fannie Mae in almost every way except for the ways that mattered most. They were working hard, but they got suspended.

Looking back on it, I know I was successful because I was fortunate to learn from the best, and I was willing to learn everything there was to know about their system. Because I was still relatively new in the business, I was able to conform to the standards they set instead of insisting on my own. This is ultimately what will enable you to master the process of not only moving REO properties, but also keeping Fannie Mae extremely satisfied with your performance.

Appendix C:

Short Sales

Can you imagine making a cold call to an "enemy" that turns into a terrific referral source?

That's exactly how I was able to list so many short sales in my market. It all started when I noticed a large billboard inviting you to call a 1-800 number and sell your home without an agent. Of course anyone telling people to sell without an agent is cutting into our business, so I decided to give the number a call to find out how it worked.

The man who owned that particular billboard turned out to be an investor who had purchased a franchise to help him flip houses. But as it turned out, he couldn't buy homes from a lot of the people who called him because their houses were upside down (they owed more on their mortgages than the value of the homes). After a great conversation, he agreed to send those folks to me to list their houses. He was a true professional and became one of my best sources of referrals. Naturally, I returned the favor when I saw a good investment opportunity that suited him.

So that was how I came to list more short sales than almost anyone in my market. I cold called a referral source and built a relationship. If you stay curious and open-minded—maintaining professionalism at all times—you never know what can happen.

But as I said, listings were just half the battle. I still had to navigate the seemingly endless obstacles to actually closing a short sale. From red tape with the bank to buyers and sellers with cold feet, I got a crash course in frustration.

I learned to move short sales not because I wanted to, but because I had to in order to survive in the market. During the late 2000's, short sales were about a third of the market, and REO's were almost another third. You had to be able to list these kinds of properties just to get the buyers to call.

When dealing with short sales, the most important thing to understand is that banks often have little incentive to move the property. At the time I got into it, banks were just as new to short sales as agents were, so none of us knew what we were doing.

Here's how a typical short sale would go: I would collect every required document, list a home, market it and reduce the price until we obtained an offer. Then I would attempt to contact the appropriate person at the bank. Sometimes they had someone in charge of short sales, other times we had to call the toll free number and talk to anyone who would listen. We would file the paperwork and then follow up with the bank almost daily.

After a few days (or months!), the bank would tell us that they were missing one document. We would turn in that document and call the next day to ensure they received it. They would tell us to please allow three days for them to receive the document and process it. We would call them back after three days, and they would say they never got it. We would resend the document, and they would again request three days. After weeks of this, the bank would explain that they closed the file because they never got all the paperwork. That would force us to resubmit everything all over again. So a property listed in January would often sit around until June. Sounds like fun, right?

The process was extremely frustrating, especially since we were doing this before the creation of the package to train Certified Distressed Property Experts to know all that was needed to process and close a short sale. Even in the event that we got all the appropriate paperwork submitted, the bank would then order a BPO (Broker Price Opinion). This could take 30-60 days to obtain and upload into their system, and even then the appraisal often came in too high. This meant the bank would refuse to negotiate close enough to the offer, and the deal would fall through.

Along the way, we finally figured out that there was a particular percentage of the original mortgage that the bank could claim from the mortgage insurance. The bank needed to net 88.3% after taxes and fees. As long as our offer got us close to 92% of BPO value, we were far more likely to get a positive response. Most of the time, I would have to cut my commission in order to close the deal and help a homeowner avoid foreclosure. But until we figured this out, it was trial and error.

Keep in mind, of course, that all these pitfalls preceded the "normal" sale process. This meant that even if we got all the paperwork turned in and approved and got a BPO that was close enough to the buyer's offer, we still had to get the buyer's loan approved. All the normal issues—home inspection, termite inspection and so on—could still kill the deal at this point. These problems are typically worse for a short sale because the former owners were struggling financially and had few incentives to maintain their property.

So now, as agents, we would face a situation where we had worked for four or even six months, and the deal could still fall through. And sometimes we ended up cutting our losses and paying out of our pockets to fix termite damage (or something similar) just to close. Between repairs and cutting commissions, it was hard to stay in business this way.

Now of course the Home Affordable Foreclosure Alternatives (HAFA) Act has mandated banks abide by certain deadlines while processing a short sale. But passing a law doesn't mean that everyone is going to comply. Many observers believe that a significant factor in delays is the effect of short sales on the bank's accounting. When a short sale closes, the bank is immediately forced to report the difference between the sale price and balance on the mortgage as a loss. On the other hand, if they hold on to the property, the balance on the mortgage may be reported as an asset, even if the client is delinquent. Add to that the complex layers of stakeholders in a mortgage that's part of a bundle, and it's easy to see why banks appear to be dragging their feet.

It's also important to remember that the actual personnel we all deal with at the bank are typically getting an hourly wage or a salary with the task of acting in the bank's best interests. Sometimes the system is just as new to them as it is to us, and they're usually handling hundreds of properties. That's why we were working around the clock to close a particular sale while the bank didn't seem nearly as motivated. All these are reasons why many short sales are now negotiated by attorneys who simply charge a flat fee on the HUD, alleviating the work and liability for the agent.

More Pitfalls

Theoretically, one of the main incentives for homeowners to proceed with a short sale is to avoid foreclosure. While they will still take a hit to their credit, the idea is that the bank will accept less than what they owe on the mortgage, and they will at least come out without a balance. This incentive is endangered, however, when the bank still comes after the homeowner for "deficiencies."

Basically, even after the bank agrees to the short sale, it can seek a judgment against the seller for all or part of the balance owed, plus interest and penalties. Even in short sales where the entire debt is forgiven, some sellers find that the forgiven debt can be counted as taxable income. Furthermore, when a deficient mortgage is sold or auctioned off, those debts become part of the package, and the purchasers can come after the seller for that money.

These discouraging developments have led some sellers to actually sue their real estate agents, because they believed they would be completely debt free after the short sale was done. They don't realize that their situation could have been much worse had they gone into foreclosure. The loss on a foreclosure can still be taxed as income, but even worse, the seller has absolutely no control of the process, including input into the sale price. Homeowners in trouble need to understand that a short sale is still the responsible way to go. If you sell your property in a short sale for $30,000 less than you owe, you are still better off than if you go into foreclosure and your home sells for $60,000 less than you owe.

Does that difference sound too dramatic? According to an analysis cited by Arthur Delany and Ryan Grim of Huffington Post Business, banks lose an average of 19% on a short sale but about 40% on a foreclosure. This is because banks may allow foreclosures to sit on the market indefinitely, losing value and leaving the owners liable for those losses.[2] Homeowners who allow a home to go into foreclosure are ultimately putting their fates in someone else's hands.

All this let me know that we had to do the best possible job educating our sellers and buyers about the short sale process ahead of time. We couldn't afford to do all the work associated with trying to sell the house only to have the deal fall through because

---

09/05/08/short-sales-banks-blockin_n_199099.html

the seller had no incentive to close or because the buyer didn't understand what to expect.

Even after working at it for months, I still closed only about 10% of my short sale listings a month. At the end of the day, the only way to make it profitable was to work as hard as I could to list as many short sales as possible. At my peak, I had about one hundred. This was sufficient to keep my buyers' agents closing enough deals to keep us above water.

With anything you do in real estate, you have to constantly evaluate your system. Is this working? How long can we expect it to last? Is this strategy sustainable, and if not, what is our exit strategy? Our short sale system was backbreaking, and I soon saw that it was not sustainable long term. You will need to ask yourself these same questions if you decide to do short sales.

Made in the USA
Columbia, SC
04 September 2017